Discipline and Discharge in the Unionized Firm

A Publication of the
Institute of Industrial Relations
University of California

Discipline and Discharge in the Unionized Firm

ORME W. PHELPS

Berkeley and Los Angeles · 1959
UNIVERSITY OF CALIFORNIA PRESS

UNIVERSITY OF CALIFORNIA PRESS
BERKELEY AND LOS ANGELES
CALIFORNIA

CAMBRIDGE UNIVERSITY PRESS
LONDON, ENGLAND

Foreword

Extensive debate over the impact of unions on wages and other conditions of employment has tended to divert attention from the far-reaching effects of unionization on the day-to-day conduct of employer-employee relations within the firm. In the unionized firm, the determination of personnel policies is no longer exclusively a managerial prerogative. Management must exercise its personnel function within the limits posed by the union contract, and, increasingly, within the framework of an accumulating body of arbitration decisions relating to the interpretation of union contracts.

In no aspect of personnel relations has the impact of unionization been more pronounced than in matters relating to the discipline and discharge of employees. Management has always regarded the right to impose discipline and to discharge a worker for a serious offense as essential to the efficient attainment of the firm's objectives; workers have tended to regard protection from arbitrary or unjustified discharge as one of the most important functions of a union. Although management in the unionized firm retains the right to discipline a worker and to discharge him for a serious offense, it exercises this right within the limitations imposed by the union contract and must be prepared to defend its decisions through the various steps of the grievance procedure.

In this careful and well-documented study, Professor Phelps analyzes the manner in which personnel practices relating to a wide range of disciplinary problems have been modified under union contracts and under the accumulating body of arbitration awards in cases involving discipline and discharge.

Orme W. Phelps is Professor of Industrial Relations at Claremont Men's College and holds a part-time appointment as a member of the research staff of the Institute of Industrial Relations, University of California, Berkeley. He has also had experience as an arbitrator.

Arthur M. Ross
Director

Preface

This is a study of the administration of industrial discipline in the unionized firm—that is, where discipline must conform to the requirements of a union contract. A very large part of the material is taken from arbitration awards. The main reason for this is the significant part played by arbitrators in defining the limits of disciplinary action under agreements which often set no standard other than "just cause." The rulings of arbitrators have produced a definite pattern, consisting of proper grounds for disciplinary action, required procedures, and acceptable penalties. Each of these in turn is qualified by such tests as the burden of proof, firm and industry practice, quality of the evidence, condonation, consistency, extenuating circumstances, and so on. The net result is a very complete set of explicit semitechnical rules for the administration of discipline, which management fails to observe at the risk of being reversed in whole or in part, with attendant costs in money and prestige. The administration of discipline under a labor agreement is quite different from what it was (or is) in the unorganized firm.

The main body of the study is based on the disciplinary awards in volumes 1-10 of *Labor Arbitration Reports* (Washington: Bureau of National Affairs, 1946–49), volume 5 of *American Labor Arbitration Awards* (New York: Prentice-Hall, 1953), and H. Shulman and N. W. Chamberlain, *Cases on Labor Relations*

(Brooklyn: Foundation Press, 1949), supplemented by a number of later cases for comparative purposes. Volumes 1–10 of *Labor Arbitration Reports* were chosen as containing the early and precedent-setting decisions, in which the principles underlying "just cause" were laid down, and divisions of opinion aired. Making allowance for the customary practice of dissent, the consensus on major issues was high, and the agreement as to what constituted the proper questions to be asked was practically unanimous. It is the latter that management should learn.

At the same time, management would be well advised to distinguish between arbitrators' "statements of principle" and their actual decisions. Arbitrators are judges, and judges worship consistency. The facts of industrial life do not permit the degree of consistency that is compatible with judicial conscience; hence it is often necessary for arbitrators to state firmly a principle which they then proceed to overturn. In doing this, they are no different from other judges in other courts, but they are closer to the parties, less protected by legal and judicial machinery, and their decisions are in practice less subject to appeal. They are therefore roundly criticized for their own inconsistency. There would be less criticism if management understood the full complex of issues facing the arbitrator in a dispute. It is one of the purposes of this study to describe the pattern in disciplinary cases so that such misunderstanding will be reduced.

This study is an outgrowth of my work as Associate Research Economist of the Institute of Industrial Relations of the University of California (Berkeley). I am especially indebted to Arthur M. Ross, Director of the Institute, and to Benjamin Aaron, Research Associate at the Institute (in Los Angeles), both of whom read the complete manuscript, made numerous suggestions, and saved me from serious errors. It goes without saying that any errors remaining are my own responsibility. I was also assisted by financial grants from the Claremont Graduate School, and am indebted to the Industrial Relations Section of the California Institute of Technology for permission to use its excellent library.

ORME W. PHELPS

Claremont Men's College
Claremont, California

Contents

TABLES

Chapter I	Industrial Discipline: Background and Pattern

The Problem of Discipline

Discipline, in one form or another, is an element of all organized activity. Its function is to maintain order by setting limits to individual behavior which may jeopardize the interests of the group. Discipline is essentially negative, operating through penalties for wrong behavior rather than rewards for right action, as in the case of incentives. With human beings, group discipline is not instinctive, as with insects and some animals. It must therefore be enforced. The manner of enforcement—raising questions of how, for what, and by whom—reacts in turn upon the morale of the organization. Justice aside, it is no easy thing to strike the proper balance between severity and leniency. In general, the answer has been cued to the needs of the system, tending toward rigor when times are difficult and toward relaxation when the permanence and prosperity of the group structure seem assured.

Theories of discipline.—There are basically three philosophies of discipline, depending on one's view of the relative weight to be given the rights of individuals versus the needs of the organization. Where the latter are overpowering (as in military systems, especially in time of war), discipline is authoritarian. In its pure form, this means that both judgment and execution are by the responsible authority, with no provision for appeal—or at most only personal and exceptional arrangements for review. Other than the mandate of obedience, there are few formal public policies governing either standards of conduct or grades of punishment. Conduct is customary, understood; adjudication prompt and final: the soldier is stripped of rank or executed, the employee fired, the son banished and cut off. All is *ad hoc,* discretionary, at the will of the chief.

If the rights of the individual are supreme on the other hand, discipline becomes anarchic. This means that the conduct of the subordinate is self-determined. He complies or fails to comply with directions as suits his view of the situation. The scholar studies or recites as the mood moves him, the child accepts or rejects parental advice, and the employee does as told or declines assignments on grounds of hazard, impropriety, or burden. The responsible authority in such circumstances either permits free choice by subordinates as a matter of policy or has insufficient power to enforce his rulings, with the result that they are challenged at will.

Whether or not life under anarchy is "solitary, poor, nasty, brutish and short," as Hobbes declared,[1] the rule of self-determination by subordinates is clearly inimical to organized activity in the customary sense of the term. Hence it is usually regarded as the antithesis of discipline. Strictly speaking, this is an error. Anarchy is a case, if a limiting case, of the possible forms of coöperative activity. All modifications of authoritarian discipline in the direction of protection of the rights of individuals are movements toward self-determination. Theoretically, a peaceful anarchy is the ideal state of society, with coercion absent and coöperation based on agreed division of duties and norms of conduct. The ethical basis for this view is the full responsibility of the individual for *self*-discipline; and in some small, highly intelligent groups, with a full understanding of problems shared by all, it may be approximated. As a practical matter, however, in the present highly organized and intensely competitive state of human affairs, it may be disregarded, other than as a standard of comparison at the opposite extreme from absolutism.

Due process.—The intermediate position is discipline by due process. Here discipline is based on a body of recognized rules

---

[1] Thomas Hobbes, *Leviathan* (London: J. M. Dent, 1943), p. 65.

and is administered under some form of juridical procedure. The key factor in this process is formality (with its accompanying characteristic of publicity). There are agreed standards of misconduct, with their main outlines in published form (statutes, codes, contracts, handbooks, and the like). Specific penalties for various classes of misbehavior are often expressly stated and made known to all within their jurisdiction. There are formal methods of charging, investigating, proving, and punishing misconduct, the absence of which to any significant degree is a denial of due process. Channels of appeal are provided, by which the accused may challenge either the accuracy of the charges or the appropriateness of the penalties. Administration of discipline is either in the hands of a disinterested third party (police and the courts) or else the final stage of appeal is reserved to someone in a judicial position (judge, arbitrator, board) with no personal obligation either to the organization or to the individual.

Discipline by due process is a long step away from the divine right of kings, the prerogatives of management, the authority of primate, parent, or teacher. It elevates the individual, and to that extent it submerges the organization as the paramount test of value. It substitutes "government by law" for "government by men," [2] even by those men whose interest in, and commitment

---

[2] The contrast between the two has been sharply defined by Winston S. Churchill in *A History of the English-Speaking Peoples* (London: Cassell, 1956), I, 175–76: "A man can only be accused of a civil or criminal offence which is clearly defined and known to the law. The judge is an umpire. He adjudicates on such evidence as the parties choose to produce. Witnesses must testify in public and on oath. They are examined and cross-examined, not by the judge, but by the litigants themselves or their legally qualified and privately hired representatives. The truth of their testimony is weighed not by the judge but by twelve "good men and true," and it is only when this jury has determined the facts that the judge is empowered to impose sentence, punishment, or penalty according to law. All this might seem very obvious, even a platitude, until one contemplates the alternative system which still dominates a large portion of the world. Under Roman law, and systems derived from it, a trial in those turbulent countries, and in some countries even today, is often an inquisition. The judge makes his own investigation into the civil wrong or the public crime, and such investigation is largely uncontrolled. The suspect can be interrogated in private. He must answer all questions put to him. His right to be represented by a legal adviser is restricted. And only when these processes have been accomplished is the accusation or charge against him formulated and published. Thus often arise secret intimidation, enforced confessions, torture, and blackmailed pleas of guilty. These sinister dangers were extinguished from the Common Law of England more than six centuries ago."

to, the success of the organization as a whole is agreed to be predominant. To a society committed to the ethic of individualism, these are great gains. From the standpoint of the organization, however, there are accompanying liabilities. It is a short and almost inevitable step from the formation and publication of a body of rules to the participation in their making by those subject to the rules—popular governments, church synods, collective bargaining. In matters of discipline especially, the interests of the individual are short run, whereas the needs of the organization are long run. A compromise may imperil the latter in periods of stress.

There are other costs as well. Due process may be and is abused. It is cumbersome, time consuming, inefficient, and annoying. Rules grow, rule interpretations multiply, precedents accumulate. Rapid shifts of policy to conform to changing conditions become more and more difficult. There are more people to consult, more precedents to consider, more vested interests opposed to change. For these and other reasons, some of them much less objective, persons in authority have tended steadily to oppose the extension of due process in disciplinary actions, on the whole with considerable success.

The Traditional View of Industrial Discipline

Industrial discipline has traditionally been both severe and irresponsible. Since the forms which discipline takes are related to the powers and functions of the system which it supports, the ultimate in punishment by private voluntary types of organization has been expulsion. However, in most private organizations such as schools, churches, clubs, political groups, families, and the like, the penalty of dismissal has generally been reserved for major crimes such as treason or disloyalty to the group. In private employment, on the other hand, it has been used indiscriminately as the solution to all sorts of offenses, major and minor, and even where no offense was charged—simply as an egregious display of power.

There have been two principal explanations of this state of things: the competitive pressures of business, and the free contractual nature of the employer-employee relationship. Both are facts of life, but the disciplinary results were nevertheless intensely irritating. There is little doubt that the promiscuous use of dismissal is one of the prime factors in the twentieth-century dissolution of employer-employee loyalties and the substitution therefor of employee self-protection through collective bargaining.

Disciplinary powers may be—unquestionably, often are—exercised unilaterally by employers with scrupulous fairness and even with generosity, but the fact remains that the privileges which the employees enjoy are by grace and not by right. They may be withdrawn at any time or exercised arbitrarily in individual cases, with no right of appeal and no rule of form or substance to which the discipline must conform. In the austere language of the legal authority, this is stated as follows:

> At common law, the usual employment relationship was a hiring at will, with either party free to terminate the relationship at any time and for any cause or without cause. The master had uncontrolled discretion in the matter of the maintenance of his working crew and almost complete authority over the services of the servant as long as the latter voluntarily retained his employment.[3]

Employee dissatisfaction with unilateral managerial control of discipline has also been aggravated by its private, arbitrary, and unsystematic character. A misdemeanor overlooked one day might become the basis for discharge the next or suspension the week following. Orderly schemes for the investigation of charges, selection of penalties, and review were rare, and if they existed, they were privately set up and administered and only the results were revealed to affected employees. How the machinery worked, what standards were employed, and the employees' rights, if any, were strict managerial secrets.

Nonunion grievance procedures.—In recent years, a few firms have introduced a form of appeals procedure which permits nonunion employees to question management decisions, but the number of these firms is small and the handicaps great. Recourse to outside authority (through arbitration) is negligible. A 1954 survey of personnel practices covering 284 companies revealed griev-

---

[3] *Discharge for Cause*, by Myron Gollub, New York State Department of Labor, Division of Research and Statistics (New York: 1948), p. 7.

ance procedures for "hourly workers not represented by union" in 61 cases (22 per cent) as against 211 firms without (74 per cent). Arbitration was provided for in 17 of the 61 companies which heard employee complaints. Salaried employees (clerical, technical, supervisory) had considerably less access to formal channels of appeal than the production and maintenance workers in the plant. Reports from 454 companies showed formal grievance procedures in effect in 39 instances (9 per cent) as against an absence of such in 404 (89 per cent). White-collar workers had access to arbitration in only 7 cases.[4]

Thus, if the sample is typical, formal channels of appeal were open to nonunion production and maintenance employees in about one out of five firms, and to unorganized clerical personnel in one out of ten. Arbitration was a possibility in 6 per cent of the cases for hourly workers, and in 2 per cent for salaried personnel.

The reasons for such a limited showing, after more than a decade of nation-wide experience with unionized grievance handling and its obvious popularity with employees, are found in employer preferences and legal limitations. Most small firms prefer to rely on an open-door policy and informal face-to-face handling of complaints by the manager or owner. Since this is a thoroughly feasible method where the group is limited in size and everyone knows everyone else well, and since there is a very large number of small companies, the prevalence of an informal disciplinary pattern is understandable. In the United States there are more than 4,000,000 firms with less than 50 employees each. Formal complaint procedures in these companies—most of them with a dozen or fewer workers—would be so cumbrous as to defeat their own purposes.

For the larger firms, on the other hand, there are serious problems of methodology and legal hazard. Nonunion grievance procedures are usually either a carry-over from an employee representation plan of the early 1930's or are designed along the new well-known multiple-step, union-management plan. In either case,

---

[4] The companies ranged in size from fewer than 250 employees to 5,000 and more, with the great majority concentrated in the range of 250 to 4,999. See *Personnel Practices in Factory and Office*, Studies in Personnel Policy, No. 145 (New York: National Industrial Conference Board, 1954), pp. 56, 109.

they call for employee participation. This can create a dilemma, if there is no employee organization to provide the machinery for selecting representatives. If management encourages the formation of such an organization, it may be committing an unfair labor practice, as defined in Sec. 8(a)(2) of the amended National Labor Relations Act, to wit: "to dominate or interfere with the formation or administration of any labor organization or contribute financial or other support to it." There is a large number of cases in which the National Labor Relations Board has so ruled.[5] The inherent contradiction involved in a management-designed plan which calls for joint action with an autonomous employee group has been enough to stop action in many cases.

If this hurdle is cleared, employee participation raises other problems. In the absence of protection by a labor agreement, many workers would just as soon not serve on grievance committees or as representatives of their grieving colleagues. It is not regarded as the sure route to "promotion and pay," especially if a vigorous presentation is called for.[6] The question of pay for time spent in such work during and after hours is also present, with both the Taft-Hartley Act and the Fair Labor Standards Act to be consulted. If arbitration is resorted to, the employer must pay for it, and once more the questions of obligation and interest are raised. Will (can) arbitration supported by one of the parties be completely impartial?[7] In the unionized situation it is customary for the costs to be split between the parties. Since arbitration is expensive, this also serves as a brake upon the indiscriminate pressing of appeals. In its absence, what limits should be placed on employees taking their complaints to the final step?

The difficulties of legality and method are imposing, but they would probably not be so effective if the opposing considerations

---

[5] See *International Harvester Co.* (1936), 2 N.L.R.B. 310; *Wyman-Gordon, Inc.* (1945), 62 N.L.R.B. p. 561; *Carpenter Steel Co.* (1948), 76 N.L.R.B. 670; and others.

[6] The many disciplinary cases going to arbitration under labor agreements, in which the prime question is the degree of independence allowable to union representatives in the plant, is some proof of the correctness of this position.

[7] This may seem a small point, to be answered promptly in the affirmative. However, the courts are rigorous in their standards of independence for arbitrators. See *Matter of Knickerbocker Textile Corp. and Sheila-Lynn, Inc.* (1939), Sup. Ct. of N. Y., 16 N.Y.S. 2D. 435.

were more compelling. The joint consideration of grievances is unquestionably a surrender of managerial prerogative. This is still very distasteful to many executives, a "compromise of principle." It gives the impression that employees have rights and that management can err. If arbitration is included, there is implied a set of rules (a "higher law") to which management must conform.[8] In addition, under a grievance procedure, management often feels impelled to think through and reduce its employment policies to writing, a task of some proportions and another limitation upon prerogative if the results are made public.

It is clear that this is a long step away from "the divine right to manage," as it has been called by a spokesman for the United Steelworkers.[9] To some managements, employee participation in the disposition of complaints looks like an open invitation to employee organization and unionism. Since management calls the shots in directing the work force and takes the responsibility for the results, it feels that it should also call the shots in judgment of the work force. The two are hard enough to disentangle, as any examination of arbitration awards will bear out. The upshot is a natural inclination to look for reasons against taking the step rather than for reasons in its favor.[10]

Industrial discipline in the personnel literature.—The disinclination of management to systematize or to make known its disciplinary procedure is clearly reflected in the literature of personnel administration, which is magnificently detailed in such matters as the methods of interviewing candidates for employment, the details of innumerable forms and records, the varieties of merit rating, the wide range of "employee services," and so on. Discipline and discharge is the blank spot in the canvas. Out of more than a dozen recent personnel texts and handbooks, published between 1949 and 1956, only four have so much as a chapter on the subject, and of these only two could be called adequate by

---

[8] As will be pointed out later, this is most definitely the case. See chap. v, discussion of "insubordination."

[9] Address by Ben Fischer at the annual meeting of the National Academy of Arbitrators, March 29, 1951, at Chicago, Illinois. See 16 LA 991.

[10] At least one arbitrator with experience in nonunion grievance arbitration has stated his opinion privately to me that "a grievance and arbitration procedure for unorganized employees simply cannot be made to work."

any standards of comparison with current industrial practice.[11] In the remainder, the topic is either omitted entirely or touched on as an unpleasant management responsibility to be exercised fairly and impartially with due regard to the needs of the firm and the morale of the workers.

The most comprehensive treatise on personnel administration in print offers the following enlightening advice, as its total contribution to the subject:

Demotions, layoffs and discharges are problems that most organizations would prefer to avoid. When they are necessary, however, the feelings of the individuals affected may be in part mitigated if the organization is in a position to justify its actions in terms of employee performance. [This means "merit rating."] If the employees affected, and others as well, realize that fairness and consideration are the keynotes of personnel policy, rather than favoritism, whim, and expediency, the "climate" of personnel relations may in some measure be improved.[12]

There is no mention of employee rights under a possible collective agreement; of any kind of appeals procedure; of union representation, responsibility, or influence; or of the standards employed in arbitration of discipline and discharge cases although hundreds of awards are publicly available in all large libraries. The treatise literature is almost equally barren, with the major personnel journals averaging less than an article a year on the problem, and most of these implying the unencumbered exercise of managerial prerogative in the assessment of penalties.

Industrial discipline under collective bargaining.—Unfortunately for this view of things, the major premise is inaccurate. In the unionized sector of the economy, at least, employers no longer have the plenary right to punish misconduct. In 19 cases out of 20 they share their authority with the union by the specific

---

[11] These are: Paul Pigors and Charles A. Myers, *Personnel Administration* (3d ed.; New York: McGraw-Hill, 1956); and G. Watkins, P. A. Dodd, W. Mc-Naughton, and Paul Prasow, *The Management of Personnel and Labor Relations* (New York: McGraw-Hill, 1950). In both books there is a good brief survey of the general outlines of a system of discipline: standards of conduct, penalties, and procedures, with some attention to the processing of appeals and resort to arbitration.

[12] John F. Mee, editor, *Personnel Handbook* (New York: Ronald, 1951), p. 283.

terms of the agreement.[13] These agreements cover approximately half of the employees in private business—between eighteen and twenty million employees directly and another three to five million indirectly (nonunion employees in unionized firms)—and their influence does not end there.[14] Collective bargaining is most prevalent in the largest firms and in the most "industrial" employments, where disciplinary requirements are most severe.[15] Any discussion of industrial discipline that omits the contractual limitations upon managerial rights and the agreed standards of good practice worked out in numberless bargaining sessions with union representatives in consideration of grievances and through referral to arbitration is therefore quite misleading.

In the typical case today, industrial discipline takes place under a union contract.[16] On the whole, it has a well-established structure and is rapidly acquiring a pattern of substantive content which defines the rights of employees both as to tenure and to the wide variety of privileges and exceptions which mark their protected status under the agreement. The main outlines of the structure are: a procedural apparatus, a code of penalties, and standards of misbehavior justifying corrective action.

Both the structure and the set of relationships which give it content are partly set forth in the contracts. However, they are much more fully worked out in grievance bargaining between unions and management, and especially in the arbitration of key issues.

Arbitration.—The professional arbitrator has become a major factor in industrial personnel administration. As the final step in the appeal procedure, he is the "Supreme Court" of industrial jurisprudence, the guarantor of due process of law to millions of employees. Arbitration awards are the main source of information

[13] In the remainder it is an open question whether or not the existence of a contract implies such a limitation.

[14] See O. W. Phelps, "A Structural Model of the U. S. Labor Force," *Industrial and Labor Relations Review*, 10 (April, 1957), 402–23.

[15] The necessity for discipline is enhanced by: size, which puts a premium on timing, coördination, delegation, and standardization of policies and techniques; and by mechanization, with its accompanying interdependence of operations, safety rules, and greater responsibility for equipment and processes.

[16] The statistical basis for "typical" as used here is a majority of employees, not a majority of firms.

about the details of personnel administration under union contract,[17] and they are *the key influence in setting rules for managerial interpretation and administration of the agreement.*

Arbitration awards are usually detailed and informative, with the reasoning underlying the decisions carefully explained.[18] Although there is by no means complete agreement among some arbitrators as to their meaning or application, in disciplinary cases a set of what might be called "juridical standards" is cited constantly in the process of arriving at both conclusions of fact and appropriate penalties.[19] These are the special contribution of the professional arbitrator, but they have undoubtedly been appropriated by employers and unions as the latter have learned to manipulate and apply them. Prominent among them are:

1. Acceptable methods of contract interpretation, derived from rules of law and equity, past practice in the firm and the industry, and the understandings between the parties.

2. Rules of evidence (including presumptions in favor of the accuser or the accused) and of confrontation, cross-examination, and special investigation.

3. The "burden of proof," which means the primary responsibility for "making a case" (establishing guilt or proving innocence).

4. Extenuating circumstances, justifying reduction or cancellation of penalties.

These "judges' rules" add a new dimension to the work of the

---

[17] The existing personnel literature is almost wholly defective as a guide to this foremost area of personnel management, being confined primarily to discussion of nonunion situations where management's prerogatives are unrestricted. Arbitration awards, on the other hand, describe a different world—one where personnel is *jointly* managed under policies negotiated by representatives of the employer and the union and set forth in an agreement giving the employees thereunder a series of enforceable rights.

[18] The most complete selection of arbitration awards is found in *Labor Arbitration Reports,* published serially by the Bureau of National Affairs. In this service the awards are carefully classified and a comprehensive *Digest and Index* summarizes the opinions therein. A more limited sample of awards, without the advantages of classification, is found in *American Labor Arbitration Awards,* published by Prentice-Hall.

[19] Most of these, of course, are of quite general application, and are not restricted to questions of discipline alone. For an excellent discussion of some of the differences of opinion with respect to these matters, see Benjamin Aaron, "Some Procedural Problems in Arbitration," *Vanderbilt Law Review,* 10 (June, 1957), p. 733, especially "Presenting the Case," pp. 738–47.

industrial supervisor. He disregards them at his own risk. Though perhaps secondary in importance to procedural requirements and the facts of behavior, they may at any time be erected into a full or partial defense to a charge of misconduct, on grounds of denial of due process.

The Right of Appeal

The appeals procedure.—The foundation stone of due process in industrial employment is the collectively bargained labor agreement, with its grievance procedure ending in arbitration. There are no reliable full-count censuses of the number of union contracts in existence, the frequency of appearance of specific clauses in agreements, or the number of grievances filed or arbitrations held per year or other period. However, the U. S. Bureau of Labor Statistics and other agencies have conducted extensive surveys to find out what goes on, and these have been supplemented by regional studies and authoritative guesses by well-informed persons.

It is officially accepted that there are more than 125,000 union contracts currently active in the United States,[20] and that formal grievance procedures are almost universally included in them. A B.L.S. study of 2,850 agreements in 1950–1951 disclosed that 94 per cent outlined formal steps for handling employee complaints and that "most of the remaining agreements referred to but did not describe a grievance procedure." [21] A detailed examination of 302 of the agreements, covering 3,400,000 workers, reiterated the details which are familiar to all students and practitioners of industrial relations.

The typical arrangement was a three- or four-step bargaining process between the union and management,[22] with arbitration at the end of the road if the parties could not settle the dispute

---

[20] "Characteristics of Major Union Contracts," *Monthly Labor Review,* 79 (July, 1956), 805.
[21] "Grievance Procedures in Union Agreements, 1950–51," *Monthly Labor Review,* 73 (July, 1951), 36.
[22] In 158 (53 per cent) of the 302 agreements, covering 2,037,000 (60 per cent) of the employees out of the total, the setup was either three-step or four-step. The full range was from a single step to some procedures with six or seven levels before arbitration. The latter were confined to a few large firms, averaging more than 10,000 employees each.

among themselves. There was a steady progression to higher levels of authority. A sample four-step progression (carefully described as "not necessarily typical") is as follows:

1. Employee or steward and foreman;[23]
2. Chief steward of department and superintendent;
3. Plant grievance committee and plant manager;
4. Plant grievance committee—national union representative and president of company or his representative.

Written statements of grievances were required in about 60 per cent of the cases, with the obvious intent of defining the controversy, making a record of dispositions at each step, and avoiding the introduction of new issues at later stages. Time limits were set in a majority of agreements for both the presentation and processing of complaints. These act as "statutes of limitations," barring the introduction of grievances after unreasonable delay, and insuring prompt movement along the path toward settlement. A minority (one-third) of the contracts required the employer to pay for the time spent by union representatives in grievance adjustment during working hours.[24] Union officials in the plant were

---

[23] The first step is often considered critically important by both management and the union. This is the level of competition for employee loyalties. If the aggrieved employee complains directly to the foreman, then management has the opportunity of making a settlement without intervention by the union. If he goes to the steward, then credit for relief accrues to the union. The union discourages individual complaint bargaining between employees and foremen, as an invitation to favoritism. Management's argument that most grievances are merely misunderstandings and easily cleared up without the necessity of formal negotiations meets the objections that the grievance procedure is a collective process supported by the organization and not the individual, that complaint settlements must conform to the agreement, and that the employee is often unacquainted with his rights and the general pattern of contract interpretation throughout the plant. The matter was urgent enough to receive attention in the Labor-Management Relations Act (Taft-Hartley), where in Sec. 9(a) it was specified that an employee or a group of employees could grieve directly to management, but the union representative must be given an opportunity to be present and any adjustment made must be consistent with the contract.

[24] An earlier BLS study of the "functioning" of grievance machinery in 101 plants reported compensation for union representatives in four-fifths of the cases and added the following significant observation: "Grievance-pay practices are very often more liberal than, and sometimes quite contrary to, the agreements. In 40 plants, some compensation is provided, but management is more liberal than the agreements specify; in 19, no reference to pay is made but wages are paid nontheless." *Monthly Labor Review,* 63 (August, 1946), 184. However, this study was conducted in wartime (1944–1945) and the situation may well have changed since then.

given top seniority ("superseniority") in a third of the contracts covering 40 per cent of the workers.

Special priorities were accorded certain types of issues, the most prominent of which was "discharge or other disciplinary action." In 37 per cent of the agreements, covering more than half of the employees, the time limits for both presentation and processing of disciplinary disputes were shortened. A third of the agreements called for by-passing either or both of the first two steps, as in the following:

If an employee represented by the Union is discharged . . . such discharge shall constitute a dispute . . . for determination under the Method of Adjusting Grievances . . . except that it must be taken up within 3 working days after the discharge, and shall be taken directly to the third step (plant grievance committee and departmental executive).[25]

Arbitration as the terminal point in grievance disposition was prescribed in 90 per cent of the agreements. This confirmed a broader study (of 1,500 agreements) a year and a half earlier, which reported arbitration clauses in more than four-fifths of the cases.[26]

An appeals procedure is fundamental to due process in industry for the simple reason that administration of the agreement is in the hands of one of the parties. Management decides what the contract means and acts accordingly. Employees who consider management's interpretation wrong can challenge its decisions through the agency of union representation. No grievance plan works perfectly, and there are plenty of opportunities for manipulation, union politics, and disagreement among employees and their union representatives as to grievances that are valid and should be pressed versus complaints that are undeserving of attention.[27] In actual operation, there are various degrees of

---

[25] *Monthly Labor Review*, 73 (July, 1951), 39.

[26] *Ibid.*, 70 (February, 1950), 160.

[27] For discussion of these points, see George Strauss and Leonard R. Sayles, "Some Problems of Communication in the Local Union," *Proceedings of the Fifth Annual Meeting of the Industrial Relations Research Association, 1952* (1953), pp. 144–46, and elaborated in their book, *The Local Union* (New York: Harper, 1953); and Van Dusen Kennedy, "Grievance Negotiation," in Arthur Kornhauser, Robert Dubin, and Arthur M. Ross, editors, *Industrial Conflict* (New York: McGraw-Hill, 1954), pp. 280–291.

informality, by-passing, and trading. Nonetheless, the complaint machinery stands as the union member's main bulwark against managerial favoritism, inconsistency, and abuse of authority. There is little doubt of its popularity with employees or of their unwillingness to forgo its orderly, systematic protection of their rights under the contract.

Grievances.—Statistics on grievances are almost entirely lacking. Nobody knows how many grievances are filed, how they are distributed by subject matter (wages, seniority, discipline, job classification, and so on), or what disposition is made of them at each step of negotiations between company and union.[28] No over-all figures are available, even as estimates, and the record of individual company experience is almost equally barren.[29] There are minor exceptions to this generalization, two of which are the following:

The Bethlehem Steel experience.—A table showing the disposition of employee complaints at various steps may be constructed from a few incomplete figures on grievance handling included in a study of arbitration in the Bethlehem Steel Company during the decade 1942–1952 (see table 1). The data on grievances are for an 8½ year period, August, 1942, to December 31, 1950, and cover the disposition of 17,000 protests filed at the first step during that time.

The data indicate that the union bargained out partial or full satisfaction in 5,050 cases (30 per cent), withdrew or dropped its complaint following denial in 9,950 cases (58 per cent), and took 2,000 (12 per cent) to arbitration. For the full decade, 1942–1952, around 20,000 grievances were filed at the first step, of which 2,400 survived to be "taken to" arbitration. However, less than half of this remainder went to a decision. Some 1,150 were withdrawn by the union and another 100 were settled by the parties. With 100 still pending at the time of the study, arbitrators' decisions were recorded for only 1,003 of the 20,000 issues originally joined, or about 5 per cent. For what it is worth, this tends to confirm a frequent guess that

---

[28] The collection of such data will be complicated by the difficulty of defining a grievance and by variations in company policy. For example, if a complaint is presented by an employee directly to a foreman—as many are—is it a "grievance"? In some cases, this is the first step; in others, it is a preliminary and the first step is where the complaint is made known to the union or reduced to writing. Many firms keep no record of grievances filed or of grievance settlements, on policy grounds. Others, who keep records, consider them confidential, and so on.

[29] Needless to say, this is a virgin and promising area for field research.

TABLE 1

DISPOSITION OF GRIEVANCES AT BETHLEHEM STEEL, 1942–1950

Disposition of grievances	Step 1	Step 2	Step 3	Step 4	Arbitration[a]	Total
Grievances filed.......	17,000	14,800	11,600	5,300	2,000	15,000
Granted...........	900	1,100	1,200	200		3,400
Compromised.......	400	600	500	150		1,650
Withdrawn[b]........	400	500	2,600	1,150		4,650
Denied...........	15,300	12,600	7,300	3,800		
Dropped[b].........	500	1,000	2,000	1,800		5,300

SOURCE: *Arbitration of Labor-Management Grievances: Bethlehem Steel Co. and United Steelworkers of America, 1942–52.* U. S. Bureau of Labor Statistics, Bulletin No. 1159 (Washington: 1954), p. 3.
[a] Not all grievances carried to arbitration were pressed to an award. Many were withdrawn or settled by the parties.
[b] Figures were supplied to make the data add up. All the other figures are in the report, except the totals. No totals are given for grievances denied, as many of them are carried to the next step and they are therefore not cumulative.

5 per cent or less of grievances go all the way to third-party adjudication.

District 31, United Mine Workers of America.—From a study of 1,053 grievance settlements between the United Mine Workers of America and coal operators' associations in northern West Virginia and western Pennsylvania between 1933 and 1954, Professor Gerald G. Somers has worked out dispositions, both by level of settlement and by subject (see table 2). The decisions thus analyzed were by no means all the grievances handled during these years; they were those surviving to the third step in the grievance machinery, which is set up in the manner illustrated below.

5.	Arbitration	⎫ The 1,053
4.	Joint Board	⎬ were at
3.	Union Commissioners–Operator Commissioners	⎭ these levels.

2. Union District Representative–Mine Superintendent

1. Mine Committee and Employee–Mine Foreman

Data for the year 1954 alone showed only 7 per cent of grievance settlements taking place beyond the first two steps, whereas 77 per cent occurred at the Mine Committee level and 16 per cent took place at the District Representative–Superintendent step. The 1,053 cases studied were therefore probably less than 10 per cent of the total, and we have no data on dispositions nearer the point of origin. For the 1,053, however, dispositions were as indicated in table 2.

Disciplinary grievances.—Since nobody knows how many grievances are filed annually or their apportionment by subject

TABLE 2

DISPOSITION, BY LEVEL OF SETTLEMENT, OF 1,053 GRIEVANCES
DISTRICT 31, UNITED MINE WORKERS OF AMERICA

Level	Granted	Denied	Compromised	Referred back	Total
Umpire.............	252	221	73	1	547
Joint Board.........	106	81	30	1	218
Commissioners.......	168	87	33	—	288
Totals............	526	389	136	2	1,053

SOURCE: Gerald G. Somers, *Grievance Settlement in Coal Mining* (Morgantown, West Virginia: Bureau of Business Research, West Virginia University, 1956).

matter, there is a like ignorance of the volume of grievances arising out of discipline and discharge. They are a significant fraction of all published arbitration awards, which might lead to the conclusion that they were an equal proportion of employee complaints. This could very easily be in error, for it fails to take into account the possibility of varying rates of attrition for different kinds of protests at successive stages of appeal. It could be argued in all sincerity that disputes over discipline were the kind most likely to be resolved by the parties without recourse to assistance from the outside—or the contrary. In the former case, the volume of arbitrations would understate the case; in the latter they would overstate it.[30]

Whichever is true, disciplinary issues show up prominently in published decisions of the umpires. They figure in roughly one-eighth of the awards reported by the Bureau of National Affairs,

---

[30] The Somers study gives some support to the latter thesis (overstatement). This analysis showed a higher percentage of discipline and discharge cases carried to the umpire than of any other type of complaint. The level of settlement for the three principal classes of grievances, comprising more than three-fourths (78 per cent) of the total, was as follows:

Classes of grievances	Level of settlement (in per cent)		
	Commissioners	Joint board	Umpire
Discipline and discharge...................	20	13	67
Claims to work (seniority)................	22	20	58
Wage or job classification................	28	25	47

No other class of grievance was taken to the umpire in more than 50 per cent of the cases.

Inc., in *Labor Arbitration Reports,* and were a factor in almost precisely one-fourth of the decisions published in volume 5 (1953) of *American Labor Arbitration Awards,* or 105 out of 415 cases.[31] There were 89 disciplinary cases in the 1,003 arbitrations between the Bethlehem Steel Company and the United Steelworkers of America in the decade 1942–1952, or 9 per cent of the awards.[32] Julius J. Manson of the New York State Board of Mediation reported in 1953 that discharge cases were the most frequent source of arbitration in the experience of that agency.[33] His testimony is supported by a check of the files of the American Arbitration Association, which indicated that discipline and discharge came first in frequency among issues, with approximately 30 per cent of the cases.[34] More than thirty years earlier, Malcolm P. Sharp reported from his experience with arbitration in the Chicago garment trades that, "the great majority of the cases which arise in the factories are cases involving routine matters of discipline. . . ."[35] Similar observations have been made by such experienced arbitrators as John A. Lapp, Clarence M. Updegraff, and Whitley P. McCoy.[36]

[31] Many arbitration awards involve two or more issues. In the count reported, all cases involving disciplinary action or discharge, whether alone or combined with other questions, were included.

[32] *Arbitration of Labor-Management Grievances* . . . , p. 3. This, however, was a special case. The overwhelming majority of the grievances settled by arbitration at Bethlehem in this period were over wage rates, job classifications, and seniority. Among them, they totaled 788 of the 1,003 cases, or 78 per cent. This concentration reflects the nation-wide program in the steel industry, initiated by an order of the National War Labor Board in 1944, to eliminate intraplant inequities by reducing the number of job classes and setting jointly acceptable standards. As a result, established job relationships were upset in a process extending over several years. Since the results could be challenged through the grievance procedure, the preponderance of this group of interrelated issues is understandable.

[33] "Substantive Principles Emerging from Grievance Arbitration: Some Observations," *Proceedings of the Sixth Annual Meeting of the Industrial Relations Research Association, 1953* (1954), pp. 136–37.

[34] Somers, *ibid.,* p. 18. In the Somers study (p. 15), there were 291 discipline and discharge grievances (or 28 per cent) out of 1,053 settlements. This is one of the rare cases where we have the distribution of actual grievances, not arbitrations, by subject matter, limited though the coverage was to the final steps of the dispute machinery.

[35] Malcolm P. Sharp, "Due Process of Law," in John R. Commons, editor, *Industrial Government* (New York: Macmillan, 1926), p. 206.

[36] See John A. Lapp, *Labor Arbitration* (Deep River, Conn.: National Foremen's Institute, 1942), p. 37; Clarence M. Updegraff and Whitley P. McCoy, *Arbitration of Labor Disputes* (Chicago: Commerce Clearing House, 1946), pp. 131–32.

Common sense supports the evidence cited. Wherever employment has the prospect of permanence, the employee naturally expects his claim to a job and the accrual of perquisites to strengthen in proportion to his length of service. In the unionized theater of industry, this claim is carefully protected by seniority rights written into the agreement. The most significant effect of discharge is that it terminates seniority and the rights which go with it. This is often a severe blow, sending the employee back to the foot of the seniority roster somewhere else. Lesser forms of discipline put an employee's record in jeopardy and often are a condition precedent to discharge. It would be strange if employees did not use the grievance procedure promptly and frequently to contest managerial decisions so inimical to their immediate as well as long-run interests.

Lloyd Reynolds appears to be quite justified in his conclusion that, "Protection against arbitrary discharge is probably the most important single benefit which the worker secures from trade-unionism. It does more than anything else to make him a free citizen in the plant." [87]

---

[87] *Labor Economics and Labor Relations* (New York: Prentice-Hall, 1949), p. 217 n.

Chapter II | Procedure

Formal procedure is the essence of due process. Paradoxical though it may sound, this is an axiom of discipline, public or private. Fair treatment of delinquents or alleged delinquents can be assured only through the requirement that the prosecutor take specific, formal, public steps to substantiate the charges brought against an alleged offender and justify the penalties imposed. The philosophical basis for ranking "form" ahead of "substance" is the purifying effect of publicity. Injustice thrives on privacy; the best guarantee of truth is the free exchange of views between accuser and accused and their representatives in an open forum.[1] No other method exists for insuring such free exchange except the insistence upon formality. This is particularly true when the administration of justice is in the hands of the accuser, as in industrial discipline.

In a discharge action initiated by the San Diego Electric Railway Company and challenged by the Amalgamated Association of Street, Electric Railway, and Motor Coach Employees of America, the company officials disregarded procedural requirements written into the agreement between the carrier and the union, holding that it was sufficient to give the employee notice with reasons at the time of firing, and that it might rely upon

---

[1] John Stuart Mill, *On Liberty* (London: Oxford University Press, 1933), chap. ii.

secret data for the discipline if it were willing to bring such data forth when the case came to arbitration. The arbitrator's reaction was emphatic:

> Sec. 18H and J are rules restricting the Company's area of discretion in disciplinary matters. Read together, the two provisions make it perfectly clear that (1) all charges of rule violations or other improper conduct must be reduced to writing and delivered personally to the employee involved; that (2) the employee must be allowed a period of three days in which to prepare and submit a written answer to the charges; that (3) only then may the written charges against him, accompanied by his written answer, if submitted, be placed in his file; and that (4) notations in his file which are more than one year old will not be considered in discipline or discharge cases. . . .
> The Company is not required to grant the substantial equivalent of a trial to each employee whom it wishes to discipline, in advance of imposing that discipline; but the Company is not permitted even to consider disciplinary action against an employee on the basis of (1) oral reports or conversations never reduced to writing or made a part of the employee's record, or (2) written reports or documents, whether or not made part of the employee's record, of which the employee has never had notice or to which he has never been permitted to reply. To assert, as does the Company, that these requirements are a "ridiculous rigamarole," is to ignore the vital importance of due process in the administration of a collective agreement.[2]

To meet the test of due process, discipline must be administered correctly. Administrative standards are drawn in the main from the rules of criminal procedure. Penalties must be based on charges, with notice and explanation to the employee and the union, preferably in advance, but in any case eventually in full. Both the charge and the incidents on which it is based must be definite and provable. Provision for protest, appeal, and a prompt hearing are indispensable. Coupled with these are "statutes of limitations," both as to the bringing of charges and the filing of grievances. The rules of evidence to be followed are broader than those applied in criminal law, with admission of hearsay and other informal data, but the allegations must be displayed in public, with an opportunity to the employee or his representative

---

[2] Benjamin Aaron, Chairman of Board of Arbitration, in *San Diego Electric Railway Co. and Amalgamated Assn. of Street, Electric Railway, and Motor Coach Employees of America* (April 13, 1948), 10 LA 119.

to explain or refute them. A full scale of remedies (erasure of reprimands, reinstatement, back pay in whole or in part) must be available to employees whose punishment has failed to meet the requirements of fair play in substance or in form.

Some of the above are derived from the "common law" of industrial jurisprudence, that is, worked out informally in the grievance procedure or laid down by arbitrators as essential to due process. Some, however, are laid down in the agreements, in the form of requirements as to:

1. The timing, notice, and explanation of charges (found in probably a majority of industrial contracts),

2. Rights of protest and appeal (practically universal), and

3. Reinstatement rights of unjustly discharged or suspended employees (appearing more and more frequently).

Since the most serious form of punishment is discharge,[3] procedural requirements are frequently coupled to that penalty.

Timing, notice, and explanation of charges.—A Bureau of National Affairs study of 400 representative agreements in 1953 disclosed that the most common notification clauses call for a written explanation of the reasons for dismissal to be handed to the employee either before or at the time of dismissal, with advance warning of one week a common practice.[4] Special discharge procedures were found in 55 per cent of the agreements, as compared with only 35 per cent three years before:

Ranging from the bare requirement of notice before firing up to provisions for prior suspension, formal hearings before discharge, and/or union participation, some kind of discharge procedure is carried in three-fifths of manufacturing contracts and two-fifths of nonmanufacturing.

In the absence of a contract provision, however, the employer still discharges without a statement of reasons at his own risk.

When a discharge case does come before an arbitrator, however, he has sometimes insisted upon some degree of pre-arbitration "due

---

[3] Although industrial penalties may be arranged in a schedule of ascending severity (see below, chap. iii), discharge is really a different order of magnitude from the rest. It is the only form of disciplinary action which constitutes a "break in service," thus wiping out seniority and other accumulated benefits.

[4] *Union Labor Report* (Washington: Bureau of National Affairs, October 16, 1953), pt. 2.

process" even though it is not specifically required by the contract. Since the deprivation of employment for alleged cause is such a serious blow to the worker, it has been thought proper and reasonable that before the drastic step of dismissal is taken, he be afforded the elementary advantage of a consultation in the sense of a confrontation with the grounds for his proposed discharge and an opportunity to reply.[5]

For example, in *Die Tool and Engineering Co. and UAW, Local 155*, the arbitrator, Dudley E. Whiting, held as follows:

Under a Company-Union contract whereby a discharge must be for cause, an employee must be informed of his discharge and the reason therefor at the time. Such was not done in this case. The management did not even inform Rasmussen that he was discharged. It did inform the Union Chief Steward of its intention to "pull his card" but did not even state the reason therefor to the committee at the time. Under such circumstances I feel that he must be reinstated.[6]

A type of prerequisite frequently written into agreements is notice to the union either before or immediately following discharge. This notice may be automatic or upon request, written or oral, and with or without time limits. For example:

In case of a discharge reasonable notice shall be given to the departmental committeeman prior to the discharge.

or

The Company agrees to notify the department steward or the Chief Steward at the time of or immediately subsequent to discharging any employee, but such notice of discharge shall in no event be given to the Union more than twenty-four (24) hours subsequent to such discharge.

or

The union upon request will be advised in writing of the reasons for any discharge.[7]

---

[5] *Discharge for Cause*, by Myron Gollub, New York State Department of Labor, Division of Research and Statistics (New York: 1948), p. 29.

[6] 3 LA 156, cited in H. Shulman and N. W. Chamberlain, *Cases on Labor Relations* (Brooklyn: Foundation Press, 1949), p. 436. This volume will hereafter be referred to as Shulman and Chamberlain, *Cases*.

[7] *Union Contract Clauses* (Chicago: Commerce Clearing House, 1954), pp. 534, 535. This publication will hereafter be cited as Commerce Clearing House, *Clauses*.

In the BNA study of 1953, the statistical frequency of each separate procedural requirement was limited, but the total was impressive.[8] Individually, the count was:

Union to be given reasons for discharge—35 per cent of manufacturing contracts and 24 per cent of nonmanufacturing.

Hearings before discharge—1/7 of the agreements, with practically all of them giving the union a voice in the discussions,

Warning prior to discharge—1/9 of contracts (often waived for serious offenses),

Suspension prior to discharge (usually for 5 days)—7 per cent of the agreements,

Formal schedule of disciplinary actions culminating in discharge (the so-called "price lists")—9 per cent of the agreements, up from 5 per cent in a similar 1950 study.

According to some agreements, employees may not be discharged at certain specified times: during the first week of employment, during vacation, before the end of a shift, during the first two hours of work, on any day but Saturday.[9] Restrictions may also be placed on lesser forms of punishment, to wit: "When it becomes necessary to discipline an employee for reasons other than discharge (*sic*), the Union Committee will be given the reason before disciplinary measure is taken."[10]

Rights of protest and appeal.—Not all disciplinary actions are appealable,[11] and where protest is permitted the procedure may be curtailed at either end. A foreshortening of the appeal means speeding up the decision, either by creating a special committee of review or eliminating the first one or two steps in the regular grievance process. Curtailment at the terminal end usually means the lack of access to arbitration if the protest is refused at the final step between the parties. Since the latter is a one-sided

---

[8] They add up to 70 per cent, exclusive of duplications, and 55 per cent with the duplications taken into account.

[9] Commerce Clearing House, *Clauses*, p. 550.

[10] Commerce Clearing House, *Clauses*, p. 532.

[11] Labor agreements in the casual trades (construction, maritime, entertainment, etc.), where employment is intermittent and of limited duration with particular employers, are much less concerned with discharge or other forms of discipline. The jobs are customarily closed shop, and the employee's security is his membership in the local union, which controls the market. Seniority with the individual employer is of no importance at all, so the impact of dismissal is much diminished.

arrangement favoring management (with a deadlock meaning that management's decision stands), the union may demand as a *quid pro quo* a specific provision in the agreement voiding the no-strike clause. For example:

> As to any dispute not subject to arbitration, no strike, work stoppage, or lockout will be caused or sanctioned until negotiations have continued for at least five (5) days at the final step of the bargaining procedure described. [This means the grievance procedure.] Thereafter any strike which occurs under such circumstances shall not be deemed to be a violation of this Agreement, which shall continue to remain in full force notwithstanding such strike.[12]

Notwithstanding the infinite variation of labor agreements as to coverage and content, it is safe to say that four out of five contracts guarantee the right of the employee to appeal a discharge and outline the formal procedures to be followed.[13] Some go much further. The most extreme degree of protection is to admit the union to joint responsibility, as in the following:

> It is further agreed by the parties hereto that no employee shall be discharged from and after the date hereof unless it is agreed to by the shop committee and/or the Union.[14]

This is unusual, although prior "discussions" are specified with some frequency. ("There will be no discharges until the matter has been discussed with the Chief Shop Steward.")[15] However, contract after contract proclaims the right of the union representative to challenge all discharges, investigate them, confer with discharged employees before they leave the plant, or accompany them to the labor relations office to hear a statement of the charges. A simple discharge procedure that covers several of the steps referred to above is found in the *Agreement between North American Aviation, Inc. and the United Automobile, Aircraft & Agricultural Implement Workers of America (UAW)*, effective March 19, 1956.

---

[12] Commerce Clearing House, *Clauses*, p. 676.

[13] This was the finding in the Bureau of National Affairs' *Union Labor Report* of 1953: right of appeal in four-fifths of all contracts, with time limits for filing in 54 per cent of the cases (within one to five days of discharge in most of them).

[14] Commerce Clearing House, *Clauses*, p. 536.

[15] *Ibid.* Needless to say, such clauses have provided a number of disputes as to the meaning of "discussion," where no agreement was reached.

Discharge Procedure

(a) When practical, employees to be discharged will be notified of this fact no later than one (1) hour before the end of their shift.

(b) If any employee is discharged, he shall be given the opportunity upon his request to present his grievance to his District Steward as provided in this Article, preferably before leaving the department and in any event before leaving the plant.

(c) In discharge cases the Union reserves the right to seek reinstatement and compensation in whole or in part for lost wages on the ground that the employee was wrongfully discharged.

(d) Grievances arising out of discharges will be initiated at the Second Step of the Grievance Procedure within the time provisions of Section 26 (a) of this Article, rather than in the First Step, by filing with the Director of Labor Relations or his designated representative.[16]

There is no standard method for processing appeals. The regular grievance machinery may be used, or a special board of review—either standing or *ad hoc*—may hear all disciplinary cases or discharges alone.[17] Accelerated handling may be prescribed for discharge complaints or for suspension-plus-discharge. Time limits may be set for the filing of protests, the employer's response, steps in the procedure, and for settlement, whether by the parties alone or through arbitration. The agreement may call for suspension as a prerequisite to dismissal:

Management agrees that an employee shall not be peremptorily discharged from and after the date hereof, but that in all instances in which Management may conclude that an employee's conduct may justify suspension or discharge, he shall be first suspended. Such initial suspension shall be for not more than five (5) calendar days.[18]

Or the contract may require that employees be kept at work until the issue is settled:

The Union shall investigate the notice of the intended discharge within forty-eight hours of the receipt of same. If the Union does not consent to the proposed discharge, the question shall be referred to the Impartial Chairman, whose decision shall be final. Pending such decisions, the employee shall continue working at full pay.[19]

In such cases, exceptions are commonly permitted in the case of

---

[16] Pp. 36–37 of the agreement.

[17] The 1953 Bureau of National Affairs study reported special appeals procedures in 27 per cent of the agreements.

[18] Commerce Clearing House, *Clauses*, p. 539.

[19] *Ibid.*, p. 543.

major offenses, as follows: "This clause will not be binding upon the Employer, however, in extraordinary cases where and when an instant discharge is absolutely warranted." [20]

At the final step in the grievance procedure, the scope of arbitration in discharge cases (or discipline cases generally) may be limited to findings of fact: that the company acted arbitrarily, that the dismissal was for proper cause, and so on. The effect of such limitations is to stop the arbitrator from ruling on the appropriateness of the penalty; he can only find the employee guilty or not guilty, whether or not he thinks the punishment unduly severe.

Reinstatement rights.—The maximum indemnity of the unjustly suspended or discharged employee is reinstatement with full back pay and seniority rights unimpaired. If decided in arbitration, the cash award may be reduced by the amount of any earnings or unemployment compensation received during the period the employee is off the payroll. This is also set forth in the contract in some cases, to wit: "If the employee is found not guilty of the charge he shall be reimbursed by the Company for all time lost less monies earned in the meantime." [21] A more usual provision, however, is the following general obligation:

In the event that such discharge is determined to have been unwarranted said employee shall be reinstated in good standing and without prejudice or loss of his seniority rights and shall receive full pay for the time lost.[22]

The obligation of the company to repay may be unlimited (as in the illustration above) or it may be restricted to a given period or amount: 30 days, four weeks, a penalty payment of $25 to $50. Figuring what an employee "would have earned" had he not been laid off or discharged presents a series of technical questions in itself. As a result, many reinstatement clauses specify how lost earnings shall be computed: the employee's "regular rate," "regular weekly earnings immediately preceding discharge," "regular pay for forty (40) hours of each work week during the layoff," "hours worked by other employees in his department," rulings

---

[20] *Ibid.*
[21] Commerce Clearing House, *Clauses*, p. 546.
[22] *Ibid.*, p. 547.

on the inclusion or exclusion of shift differentials and overtime, and so on.

Employees "properly" discharged for cause are also not without their rights, and these may be set forth in the agreement. The most common are vacation allowances which have been earned in whole or in part and accumulated severance pay. Here the cause of discharge may be influential, as indicated in the clause set forth below:

> If an employee fails to challenge dismissal for gross misconduct or if subsequent hearings through the grievance procedure result in the dismissal being final, the employee shall forfeit all rights to terminal vacation and notice and severance pay.[23]

It is hard to keep a code of procedure from becoming complicated. In some agreements, reinstatement rights carry the qualifications that employees restored to their jobs as a result of improper discharge must pay back to the employer any vacation or termination allowances received at the time of separation.

The right to reinstatement with pay and privileges unimpaired as recompense for improper dismissal has been held by arbitrator after arbitrator to be implicit in the employer's obligation to discharge only for proper cause. It is nonetheless (or perhaps "therefore") a popular provision in the agreements. The BNA study of 1953 reported that 49 per cent of the contracts analyzed specified reinstatement of employees unjustly dismissed, with full back pay automatic in 3/5 of the cases. Back pay was limited in 1/5 of the agreements, and in the remainder the matter was left up to the arbitrator.

Discharge is "economic capital punishment"—the maximum penalty the employer may assess against the employee. Although of less urgency, discipline short of discharge is also of concern to employees and to the union, and has been the subject of a number of contractual limitations. For certain classes of misconduct, some agreements forbid discharge at the first offense. Others set a graduated series of penalties (warnings, reprimands, suspensions, and the like), depending on the gravity of the fault or prior misconduct; still others require prior notice to and/or

---

[23] *Ibid.*, p. 549.

discussion with the union or specify exactly what a given form of punishment means. Contrasting treatment of seniority rights during suspension, for example, are illustrated in the cases below:

When suspended, an employee loses all rights to wages during the period of suspension, but does not lose his other employee rights and benefits.

The time during which an employee shall have been laid off on account of personal fault shall be deducted from his aggregate service record.[24]

The growth of contractual definitions of employee rights in discipline and discharge cases has been rapid and is practically certain to continue. Most of the clauses which now define "just cause" or which set explicit procedural rules were unknown half a generation ago. The major pressures have come from the forced growth of grievance procedures ending in arbitration during World War II (as a result of War Labor Board orders), the coupling of "cause" with the right to discipline and dismiss in managerial prerogative clauses, and the referral of disputes arising thereunder to the grievance machinery. The ensuing decisions have seldom been uniformly acceptable to both sides, and the desires of both employers and employees to correct what they considered as unwise or unjust outcomes and to perfect the adjustment process has led both parties to suggest corrections and improvements. Since few agreements are complete in this respect and since ideas of employee rights of tenure and due process are spreading rapidly, further elaboration of this section of the agreement pattern may be looked for.

A recent example.—An example of the trend toward codification may be found in the *Agreement between Southern Counties Gas Company of California and International Chemical Workers Union, Locals 47, 53, 58, 66, 78, 224, 350 and 404,* April 1, 1956. Article XII, "Disciplinary Conditions and Procedures," consists of three sections: "Causes for Discipline," "Advance Warning of Intention to Discipline," and "Procedure in Discharge, Demotion and Disciplinary Lay-Off."

The "Causes for Discipline" are listed in nine groups:

---

[24] *Ibid.*, p. 552.

A. Failure to perform work in an efficient and workmanlike fashion.

B. Absence without authority and without satisfactory excuse.

C. Failure to coöperate with supervisors and/or fellow employees. . . .

D. Unsatisfactory accident record; carelessness or negligence on the job . . . unsafe, unlawful driving.

E. Insubordination—failure to comply with Company rules which have been posted or which are common knowledge . . . or of which the employee has been directly notified orally or in writing; failure to comply with orders or instructions . . . by supervisor.

F. Insobriety—drinking on the job; drinking off the job in an amount affecting the employee's attendance or quality of work.

G. Dishonesty—regarding money, falsification of reports or records, or truthtelling.

H. Grave Offenses—conviction of a felony or use of narcotics; criminal acts; immoral acts; proof of membership in the Communist Party or failure to disavow such if charged by a duly constituted legislative committee.

I. Subversive Activity—advocacy of the overthrow of the government by force and violence; commission of or conspiracy to commit sabotage; any other subversive activity.

"Advance Warning of Intention to Discipline" is guaranteed to employees charged with incompetence (Group A above). They must be notified in writing by the supervisor of the reasons for his recommendation and "where circumstances permit" will be given a probationary period to bring their work up to standard.[25] An employee so warned has the privilege of asking reclassification and transfer back to work he has previously performed successfully, if the request is made before probation ends. Or the employee may waive probation and demand an immediate hearing on the charge, "in which case his employment and pay will continue until the Company has stated its position" and the matter is either settled or goes to arbitration. A warning of unsatisfactory work dies at the end of six months if not acted upon, or earlier if the employee brings his performance up to standard.

---

[25] This is contractual recognition of the widely recognized managerial theory of "corrective discipline" in which the purpose of the action is aid and encouragement rather than retribution. Corrective discipline is not necessarily restricted to cases of unsatisfactory performance; it is also the philosophy underlying graduated penalties for various kinds of misconduct, but it is particularly appropriate to a fault connected with ability, and carrying no reflection upon personal reliability or morals. See below, pp. 45, 60-61, 72, 78, 141, 142, for further discussion of corrective discipline.

The key section is the special procedure to be followed in all cases of discharge, demotion, or disciplinary layoff.[26] To be an "immediate cause of discharge," an offense must have been committed or discovered within the preceding six months.[27] Prompt notification in writing on special forms is the first step. For discharge, the notice must give the reason for "removal from work" (which precedes actual "termination of service"), the nature of the offense (its classification among the causes for discharge), the effective date of dismissal, and the last date upon which a protest may be registered, which is five days after removal from work. If the employee requests, the Personnel Department will arrange a hearing within two to five business days (Saturdays, Sundays, and holidays not counted) and no discharge is final until such time has elapsed.

The employee may appear in person at the hearing, whether he represents himself or is represented by the union. At the conclusion of the hearing, the company notifies the employee by registered mail of its decision, and if the protest succeeds he is restored to his job with back pay for the time lost. If denied and the judgment is disputed, the matter goes to arbitration within twenty calendar days. An employee discharged for serious cause (E, F, G, H, and I above) loses his terminal pay and vacation allowance, but gets his earned holiday credits.

Both demotion and disciplinary layoff may be protested in the same way and have the same guarantees of restoration of status and pay as discharge. However, a demoted employee has an additional option. If charged with one of the milder reasons for discipline (incompetence, absenteeism, non-coöperation, bad accident record), he may elect as an alternative to demotion to resign and take his termination pay (one week's pay per year of service, up to a maximum of ten years) plus any vacation and holiday credits he has coming. This election takes the place of a protest, or if a protest has been filed, may be substituted therefor before the five-day limit is up.

---

[26] This is not a part of the regular grievance procedure, but is administered separately.

[27] This does not rule out consideration of the whole record of prior service, either good or bad, but provides "a period of time during which an employee may clear his record of an immediate cause of discharge" and a discharge action must be directly related to an offense or offenses occurring during that interval.

Temporary employees and regular employees serving their probationary period of six months are excluded from the procedure, with the company retaining the final say on whether they stay or not and in which job. However, the company agrees to "discuss" with the union any claim made in writing that a probationary employee has been unfairly dismissed and also undertakes to notify any of them who have worked three months or more of any grounds for dissatisfaction which need correction. Neither of these concessions creates any rights of tenure for such employees, however.

Good faith and the burden of proof.—There is probably no such thing as the perfect disciplinary procedure, whether described in the agreement or worked out informally by the parties. The diversity of need, method, and personality in industry is too broad to be encompassed by any single set of standards, whether of substance or of form. The true essentials of proper discipline are fair dealing and mutual trust. Both are personal attributes, incapable of guarantee or enforcement.

If a foreman and an employee dislike each other, there are a score of ways either can harass the other without formally violating any rule of good conduct. If the relationship of the company and the union is one of antagonism and search for mutual advantage, no grievance procedure will iron out the handicap. The correct machinery for disposing of the unpleasant tasks of correction and punishment is one that fits the needs of operation and satisfies the parties. It may be wholly informal, and in many small firms such an arrangement is entirely feasible. However, as the organization increases in size, some formal safeguards are called for.

The minimum formality is to recognize publicly that discipline and discharge will be for cause. This may seem to change nothing at all, for it has been the experience of millions of employees without any such protection that good performance entitles a man to his job and fair treatment. Nonetheless, formal recognition of a principle in the context of an agreement does not leave things as they were before.[28]

---

[28] The contract of employment is in fact modified substantially, from an agreement terminable at the option of either party to one terminable at the will of the employee, but by the employer only for cause. See *Discharge for Cause*, p. 11 n.

The prime effect of the phrase "for cause" has been procedural. It puts the burden of proof on the employer for any corrective action prejudicial to the employee. In nonlegal language, this means simply that the employer must prove that discipline is justified instead of the employee having to prove that it was arbitrary, inconsistent, or unfair. The difference is important; it puts the employer or his representatives on trial, with the employee presumed innocent until shown to be guilty.

The burden of proof lies with the party who asserts the affirmative of the issue. The person who asserts the affirmative is ordinarily seeking to bring about a change of circumstances. Consequently under the most usual type of clause where provision is made that discharge may occur only for just cause, the employer is seeking to bring about a change of circumstances in that he wishes to remove an employee from his job. The employer, therefore, would appear to have the burden of proof.[29]

In the nature of things, the rule of "burden of proof" is not stated in the agreement between the company and the union, but it has become the fundamental rule of fair play to millions of employees working under union contracts in the United States.

In general, procedural requirements are a guarantee of review and reconsideration, if necessary, at every step of the disciplinary process. None of them is a handicap to the employer acting in good faith; they are simply a codification of the practice in effect wherever fair play is observed. On the other hand, they almost automatically bring to light the exceptional arbitrary decision or act that violates the canons of right conduct, thus safeguarding the dignity of the employee as a person and an industrial citizen. This is the justification for their strict observance and their incorporation into the contract between the employer and the union representing his employees.

---

[29] *Ibid.,* p. 14.

Chapter III | Penalties

A major flaw in the administration of industrial discipline in the past has been management's carelessness in the selection of penalties, and particularly the indiscriminate use of dismissal. This is borne out by the most cursory examination of arbitration awards, in which "modification" of the punishment to some lighter sentence is found almost as often as the upholding of management's action, especially in discharge cases. The rule to which arbitrators subscribe is "make the punishment fit the crime." This is now the standard for management to observe, and a properly graduated code of penalties is an important element in the disciplinary pattern.

These penalties are now well standardized and innovations are discouraged.[1] The normal category of permissible chastisement is about as follows, in the order of ascending severity:

1. Simple oral warning, not of record.
2. Oral warning, noted in the employment record.

---

[1] The days of floggings and imprisonment on bread and water are over, even on the high seas, but very minor restraints outside the ordinary run the risk nowadays of being labeled "cruel and unusual" and therefore illegitimate. An example is management's suspension of an employee "until he was ready" to wear his safety goggles. The indefiniteness of the punishment was found to be a challenge to the employee's pride ("If he gives in too quickly, he may be considered a weakling.") and the employee was therefore reimbursed for three of the four days he stayed away. Award of Arbitrator Charles C. Killingsworth in *Bethlehem Steel Co. and United Steel Workers of America* (1951), 5 ALAA 68, 943.

3. Written reprimand.

4. Suspension (disciplinary layoff) for a stated period.

5. Withholding of benefits customarily accruing with the lapse of time: merit increases, promotions, etc.

6. Demotion.

7. Discharge.

There are also some penalties that are ordinarily not within management's reach, but that may be applied by disinterested parties such as arbitrators. Most prominent among these are:

8. Reduction or cancellation of seniority.

9. Requirement of resignation from office in the union for a stated period.

The type and variety of penalties to be used, as well as the manner in which they are to be employed, may be limited by contract. This may be done explicitly in a section of the agreement reserved for that purpose, as follows:

There shall be four separate penalties applied when it is necessary to inflict discipline upon any of the employees of the Company, namely:

Personal reprimand by the foreman . . . in the cases of minor offenses.

Letter of warning shall be given an employee together with oral reprimand in relatively serious cases and copies of same shall be filed with the employee's service record. . . .

Suspension from work without pay with a written notice for a period varying from one to fifteen days. . . .

Extreme penalty or dismissal from service: To be applied in all cases of flagrant violations of the rules of the Company, or the law of the land. . . .[2]

Or the definitions may be distributed more casually throughout several articles of the compact:

Three written reprimands within one twelve-month period shall be considered just cause for dismissal. . . .[3]

No officers or members of the Union Wage Committee shall be discharged except for neglect or incompetency or misconduct.[4]

In cases of first offense or infraction of minor rules, warning slips

---

[2] Commerce Clearing House, *Clauses,* p. 551.

[3] *Ibid.,* p. 529.

[4] *Ibid.,* p. 531.

will be issued to the employee by the foreman with a copy of said warning slip to be provided to the Union Shop Steward and the Personnel Department.[5]

A "price list" may be written into the agreement or included by reference, and shop rules issued separately are often brought under the contract.[6] An excerpt from one proposed price list is as follows:[7]

Rules	First offense	Second offense	Third offense	Fourth offense	Fifth offense
Gambling or engaging in lottery...	Discharge				
Leaving plant during shift.......	1 day off	1 week off	Discharge		
Mistakes due to carelessness......	Warning	3 days off	1 week off	Discharge	
Violating a safety rule...........	Warning	1 day off	3 days off	1 week off	Discharge

There is wide disagreement over the desirability of such graduated codes of penalties, but the major pressures seem to be favorable to their use. In their defense are cited the obvious advantages of standardization and consistency, which are hard to arrive at otherwise in a big plant or a big firm with several plants. If agreed to by the union, a price list also has an odor of legitimacy which may be lacking in the individual judgments of foremen, superintendents, and labor relations officers. A number of arbitrators and other authorities have approved codification of penalties and offenses, presumably on the basis of certainty and the resemblance of industrial discipline to the administration of a criminal code.

Opposition to a codified disciplinary procedure is based on the argument for flexibility of treatment under widely varying circumstances and the feeling that the undoubted rigidities of a code make "corrective" action less possible and considerably less likely. For example, if the penalty chart calls for one warning and then discharge, should management apply these sanctions equally

---

[5] *Ibid.*, p. 550.

[6] "Shop rules as attached hereto are to be part of this agreement, as well as such future shop rules as may be adopted by the Company after agreement with the Union." *Ibid.*, p. 527.

[7] Lawrence Stessin, "How to Spell-Out Your Discipline Rules," *Mill and Factory*, 58 (January, 1956), 75–79.

against the new employee and a man with twenty years of service? It may also be forgotten in reading the precise wording of a rule that violations are not always clear-cut and that circumstances may either be extenuating or demand very stringent reprisals for the same kind of offense. Insubordination is a case in point, ranging from dilatory handling of a misunderstood order to felonious assault upon a supervisor. Management fears that if it relaxes the code procedure in some cases, it faces the possibility of estoppel later on when it carries out the letter of the law.

Simple oral warning, not of record.—An oral admonition by a supervisor is prejudicial to an employee's standing and may be entered in evidence against him later on. However, as a basis for proof it is infirm, being subject to a number of defenses. It may be and often is intended as instructional, at least partly, and can be so understood by the employee with no recognition of its disciplinary import. It can be denied as a question of fact, and the problem is one man's word against another's. Its content and vigor of expression are the more questionable the longer ago the incident occurred, with consequent reflection upon the seriousness of the subject matter. A large part of any supervisor's time is taken up with advice, instruction, caution, and reprimand. These take all sorts of forms and mean many different things, both to the speakers and their audience. A violent outburst by one foreman may mean less than a quiet comment from another. Oral warnings are therefore likely to be discounted as proof unless noted in the employee's record.

Oral warning, noted in the employment record.—A notation that the employee has been warned, on the other hand, avoids the charge of evidence manufactured after the fact and singles out the misdemeanor from the usual welter of incidents in the day's work. As a strictly practical matter, it supports the case against the employee when, although:

many of the infractions of Company rules, if taken by themselves singly, would clearly not merit the drastic penalty of discharge, such infractions are of sufficient seriousness when considered as part of a consistent pattern of behavior as to become a matter of serious consequence to the best interests of the Company's employer-employee relations. . . .

In this case, the discharge was based on the employee's

repeated chronic tardiness, his frequent failure to return on time to his machine after lunch and rest periods, his habit of leaving his job station without proper permission of his supervisor, which resulted in spoilage of work and loss of work time by his teammates who were dependent upon his lead production, and his failure to maintain minimum production standards for his machine unit.[8]

Among the items submitted in evidence in this case were eight warnings issued orally by supervisors with formal notations in the employee's service record.[9]

Written reprimand.—The written reprimand goes a step further than the oral warning. It customarily originates from a different source—department head, superintendent, or labor relations office —and being in writing is more "official" and is expected to impress the recipient more than its spoken counterpart.[10] It often puts the employee on notice of the consequences of a repetition. The written reprimand is a definite black mark and may be challenged by the employee through the grievance procedure. If the challenge is successful, the reproof is expunged and the employee's record cleared of that particular demerit.

However, the written reprimand is a formality and as such must be employed consistently if at all. Once adopted as a procedure, it is disregarded at the employer's peril. One of the "judges' rules" introduced by arbitrators to insure consistency of treatment is the principle of condonation. How it works is well described in the following excerpt from an award:

---

[8] Arbitrator Harry H. Rains in *Revlon Products Co. and Distributive, Processing, and Office Workers of America, CIO* (1953), 5 ALAA 69,334.

[9] E.g.: 10/7/52—Employee was warned again this date for failure to make the production rate for unit #4 on October 6, 1952. [Signed] W. Brothers.

2/20/53—Employee was warned this date for standing and talking to another employee at 8:05 A.M. outside his work area. He was informed that it is his duty and obligation to be at his work place at 8:00 A.M., and the next violation will result in discharge. [Signed] W. Brothers.

[10] Example taken from the Revlon Products case cited above:

April 2, 1952—Please be advised that on March 28, 1958 you reported to work place late from lunch. This is in violation of working regulations. Your attention was called to this by both your supervisor and the Personnel Manager. It will be necessary for you to correct this condition or expose yourself to further disciplinary measures. [Signed] W. Crosby.

CC. Mr. Rock, Mr. Schute, Supervisor

A warnings system has several purposes. . . . Miller conceded that he had on various occasions received verbal "spankings" from supervisors, but these are not the same as written warnings. We are not impressed by Company testimony that the reluctance of supervisors to issue written warnings should be taken into account in evaluating the record. The Company must either use its warnings system or abandon it, and supervision's laxness cannot condone not using the system on appropriate occasions, if it is to remain. Where a warnings system is in effect, the workers have a right to be warned, and they may well feel that the misbehavior which is known to management but which is not followed by a warning is not regarded seriously by management. To discharge a man without a previous warning may amount to a denial of procedural "due process." We believe, therefore, that the Company's failure to follow its own disciplinary procedures makes its action in discharging Miller improper.[11]

Suspension.—A suspension is a disciplinary layoff. It may be for a very short period (the rest of the day) or for stretches up to several weeks or months, but unless expressly so provided in the agreement does not prejudice the employee's accumulation of seniority rights and other benefits. In the typical case, work and pay stop while other contract rights continue to accrue.

The extreme flexibility of suspension as a penalty imposes on the employer a special responsibility for consistency of treatment. The proper rule is to adjust the layoff to the seriousness of the offense; variations to fit the convenience of the company are a violation of this principle. For example, in the following case, it was brought out that it had been customary in the plant to lay off employees when they reported back to work, if they had been absent the day before without notice or valid excuse. However:

Testimony at the hearing disclosed the fact that foremen do not apply the penalty with any uniformity. If work is available but not urgently needed, the penalty may be imposed. But if work is available and urgently needed, the penalty is not applied. This means that whether or not a man gets the penalty is dependent solely on the foreman's estimate of the urgency of production needs. A penalty applied in this way may be understandable strictly from a production point of view,

[11] Arbitrator Emanuel Stein in *Matter of Pyrene Manufacturing Co.* (1948), 9 LA 787, cited in Robert E. Mathews, editor, *Labor Relations and the Law* (Boston: Little, Brown, 1953), p. 524. See also *Discharge for Cause*, by Myron Gollub, New York State Department of Labor, Division of Research and Statistics (New York: 1948), pp. 38–39, for further discussion of condonation as a matter of adequacy of warning.

but it is bound to be discriminatory. It is a fundamental principle that the penalty should fit the crime and not be dependent on extraneous circumstances.[12]

In the same case, the arbitrator pointed out another problem—mitigating circumstances. The indiscriminate application of a one-day suspension made no distinction between the chronic absentee, the occasional absentee, and the man with an otherwise perfect record. He suggested that the parties try to agree on criteria which would distinguish a chronic absentee from an employee with a satisfactory record.

Suspension should be for a stated period. An indefinite layoff is likely to be found a violation of the employee's seniority rights. It thus stands a good chance of being regarded as inappropriate, no matter how serious the offense of the employee. For example:

> Since the company did not avail itself of the opportunity to discharge McDonald for his absences, insubordination, and lack of industry, these factors cannot be relied upon by the company for the purpose of laying him off in connection with a decrease in the working force. They are not the factors which the contract provides shall determine who is to be laid off . . . the seniority provisions of the contract provide specifically in what order workers should be laid off.[13]

In the main category of disciplinary remedies, suspension follows warnings and reprimands, but precedes discharge. It is a flexible and powerful deterrent, in its more extended versions giving a serious foretaste of the ultimate penalty of discharge. As such, it may be challenged by the employee on grounds of lack of cause, inappropriateness, or undue severity. If the grievance is sustained, the remedy is return to the job with back pay for time lost in whole or in part.

Withholding of benefits: merit increases, promotions, and the like.[14]—Optimistic anticipations are as much a part of industrial

---

[12] Arbitrator W. E. Simkin, in *Bethlehem Steel Co. and United Steel Workers of America* (1947), 7 LA 483.

[13] Arbitrator Joseph Brandschain, in *Bethlehem Steel Co. and United Steel Workers of America* (1945), 5 LA 578, cited in Shulman and Chamberlain, *Cases,* p. 185.

[14] There is some question whether this group should be included in a "standard category" of penalties. However, benefits *are* withheld, the withholding is regarded by employees and some arbitrators as punishment, and it is subject to grievance. The classification is therefore included, for purposes of completeness.

employment as of any other form of activity. The loss of either a pay increase or assignment to a better job is a material disappointment, a blow to self-esteem, and a handicap for the future. Both are disputed regularly by aggrieved employees. And although the advancement of employees is generally considered an exercise of managerial prerogative, the agreements have imposed numerous limitations upon free choice in these respects. Promotional rights particularly have been secured for senior employees, sometimes without exception but more often with "ability and fitness" provisos, as follows:

The parties recognize that promotional opportunity and job security in event of promotions, decrease of forces, and rehirings after layoffs should increase in proportion to length of continuous service. . . .

In recognition, however, of the responsibility of Management for the efficient operation of the works, it is understood and agreed that in all cases of:

1. promotion . . . the following factors as listed below shall be considered; however, only where factors "a" and "b" are relatively equal shall length of continuous service be the determining factor:
    a. ability to perform the work
    b. physical fitness
    c. continuous service[15]

The withholding of benefits for which the employee is eligible raises a number of questions. It is a negative form of discipline in that what is done is an omission rather than an act of commission. This puts the burden of proof on the employee to show that he has been discriminated against.[16] On the other hand, if the contract gives preference in promotion to employees with both seniority rights and "the ability and physical fitness" to perform the work, what are good reasons for passing over the man with the longest continuous service? For example, is a moderate record of absenteeism or tardiness sufficient excuse? Neither is related to physical capacity or ability to perform. However, they do indicate unreliability, and management might well take the position that

---

[15] *Agreement between Manufacturing Division, United States Steel Company and the United Steel Workers of America*, August 15, 1952.

[16] When an employee is *not* promoted or has *failed* to get a pay raise, there has been no change of circumstances and it must be established that a right to advancement has been violated.

an employee so addicted is not proper material for increased responsibility.

The employee's position is equally understandable. The stigma attached to being passed over is clear and unmistakable. He loses ground relatively to other employees, and his future is jeopardized. Failure to contest the issue is admission of guilt. No matter how positive management may be, no form of evidence is more subjective than the grounds for managerial judgments of competence and capacity. A glance at any merit-rating blank will verify the subjective character of the elements to be considered, for example: judgment, coöperation, initiative, personality, human relations, and the like. Definitions are difficult, the weights vary, many of the characteristics are contradictory. The steady extension of seniority through collective bargaining is clear proof of widespread doubt of managerial competence and/or fairness.[17]

Loss of promotion and/or pay increases is not the only form of denial of benefits. Now and then management withholds holiday pay, overtime work, vacation pay, and so on, from employees guilty of minor rule violations. Holidays, particularly, are often hedged against absenteeism in the contract, as in the following example:

Straight time shall be paid to the employees if there is no work to be performed on said holidays, provided the employees work the working day before, and the working day after each such holiday.[18]

---

[17] The arguments above assume honesty and sincerity on the part of supervisors who make the ratings and recommendations. As anyone with the slightest experience in industry knows, the assumption is frequently invalid. Foremen have likes and dislikes, and interests of their own to protect. It is not unknown for a supervisor to hold back an employee from promotion to keep from losing a valuable member of his production team. The extensive use of "merit rating," in spite of its acknowledged weaknesses, is in itself a judgment on the reliability and accuracy of supervisory recommendations. "Plant politics" is an old story. The struggle for preferment is as keen in the shop as in the office and the executive staff. This helps to explain the overwhelming preference of rank-and-file employees for the impersonality and certainty of seniority.

[18] Commerce Clearing House, *Clauses*, p. 160. There are a number of variations of this clause, such as the requirement of one or more day's work during the holiday week, "perfect attendance" during the calendar week in which the holiday occurs, and so on. However, the "before and after" requirement is rather common, with its intent to protect against "stretching."

Denial of holiday pay under these circumstances has been called "non-disciplinary" by some arbitrators. To the employee, however, it is still a penalty for absenteeism and as such is subject to grievance procedure and arbitration.

When thus covered in the agreement, the penalty raises few problems. However, without a contract provision, the principle is open to question. For example:

Holiday pay and other "fringe" elements are usually considered as part of an employee's annual compensation, as his normal due, and not as a gift, whereby the deprivation thereof may be considered in the nature of a penalty or punishment for some infraction or default.[19]

Demotion.—Demotion is a limited form of disciplinary action, in that usually the cause must be related to job performance.[20] Generally speaking, an employee may not be demoted for misconduct.

It appears that arbitrators will not permit management to use demotion as a form of discipline *unless the agreement specifically provides for such.* It was held in one case, for instance, that management did not have the right to use temporary demotion as a means of discipline for negligence in job performance (as opposed to lack of ability to perform the job), where such discipline was not provided for specifically by the agreement and where the senior's position was temporarily filled by a junior employee in contravention of the seniority clause.[21]

If physically not qualified or unable to do the work satisfactorily, a man may be transferred to a lower rated job in line with his capacities.[22] This may be specified in the agreement as follows:

Employees may be downgraded to lower rated jobs only for the following reasons:
(1) For unsatisfactory performance on the employee's present job.
(2) In the event continued performance of the employee's present job will injure the health of the employee.
(3) In the event there are changes in production methods, production schedules or changes in the method of doing the job, which . . . materially change the work performed . . . to such an extent that . . . [it] falls within the job description of a lower rated job.[23]

---

[19] Arbitrator George A. Gorder, in *John Deere Tractor Co. and United Farm Equipment Workers* (1947), 9 LA 21.

[20] This means that strictly speaking it may be defined as "nondisciplinary." See discussion of incompetence and misconduct below, chap. iv.

[21] (Italics mine.) Frank Elkouri, *How Arbitration Works* (Washington: Bureau of National Affairs, 1952), pp. 250–251. Some agreements do so provide, as mentioned previously.

[22] If a reduction of force is caused by lack of work, demotions may occur, but this is nondisciplinary reassignment and seniority rules.

[23] Commerce Clearing House, *Clauses*, p. 493.

or

An employee whose performance on his present job is unsatisfactory may be downgraded to a lower rated job without respect to his seniority standing. . . .[24]

Demotion may be a right as well as a penalty. Promotional clauses frequently carry the proviso that employees unable to meet production standards in the new job may be restored to their former positions after a trial period, without loss of seniority.

Discharge.—Discharge is the ultimate penalty and in employment with any prospect of permanence the one most strenuously resisted.[25] The primary reason is that it constitutes a break in service and wipes out accumulated seniority. It is not the only form of service break—there are several kinds of both voluntary and involuntary terminations of employment[26]—but it is the most unpleasant of them because of its involuntary and derogatory nature. The three major classes of involuntary separation have been distinguished as follows:

Now a discharge is a derogatory termination because the employee has not been satisfactory. A layoff is a termination without prejudice because of insufficient work opportunity; ordinarily the laid off employee retains seniority standing for a time. Compulsory retirement fits neither of these definitions. The retired employee is terminated even though his work may have been satisfactory in every respect, and even though his job may still be active.[27]

---

[24] *Ibid.*, p. 493.

[25] In the casual trades (construction, maritime, etc.), grievances over dismissal are more infrequent than in "factory" work and other employment of a permanent nature. Nevertheless, they occur. See C. P. Larrowe, *Shape-Up and Hiring Hall* (Berkeley and Los Angeles: University of California Press, 1955), pp. 160–161.

[26] Seniority shall be broken and the employee terminated for the following reasons:

a. if the employee quits;

b. if the employee is discharged for a justifiable reason;

c. if the laid-off employee fails to report to the Employment office for a work assignment within three (3) working days after receiving notice by registered mail . . .

d. if any employee fails to keep Management notified of his proper address and by such failure the Management is unable to contact the employee by registered mail;

e. if the employee is laid off for longer than two (2) years;

f. if the employee retires or is retired. . . .

Agreement between North American Aviation, Inc., and the UAW-CIO, December 20, 1954.

[27] Arbitrator Arthur M. Ross, in *S. H. Kress & Co. and Retail Clerks Intl. Assn., Dept. Store Employees' Union* (1955), 25 LA 77.

Arguments to the contrary, notwithstanding, discharge has a definite place in any program of "corrective discipline" as a deterrent.[28] Unless the whole theory of "making the punishment fit the crime" is wrong, the possibility (or certainty) of discharge for specified forms of misconduct is a deterrent to employees who wish to keep their jobs. Dismissal is likewise presumably a "correction" to the employee who is terminated, if it is accepted that people can learn from their mistakes and that employees who are discharged do not pass forever from the labor market. The fact that discharge is hedged about with restrictions, limitations, and formalities is simply a recognition of its importance to the employee in a contract pattern where more and more benefits are deferred (anticipatory) and dependent upon the accumulation of a service record: merit increases, promotions, choice of shifts, longer vacations, guaranteed wages, pensions, and so on. In the typical industrial agreement, these are related to service with one firm. Their loss may be an economic disaster to the worker.[29]

As a rule, however, arbitrators are quite reluctant to sustain a discharge, for the deprivation of employment is tantamount to "economic capital punishment." The loss of a job by a man who depends upon it for the means of livelihood for himself and his family can be a

---

[28] The contrary view has been stated by H. T. Gierok, an officer of General Motors Corporation, in describing the operating of the umpire system in that company:

The Umpires have adhered to a philosophy called "corrective discipline." Briefly this philosophy is:

The purpose of discipline is to obtain compliance with Shop Rules, i.e., to correct improper conduct. It should not be punitive in nature; i.e., it is not to "get even" with the employee.

Discharge is a disciplinary action which is not "corrective" in nature. Therefore, discharge should be resorted to in two types of situations:

Where the offense is of such serious nature as to make any other form of discipline inadvisable.

Where other efforts to bring about correction have failed.

Cited in Paul Prasow, "An Examination of the Role of Arbitration Principles in an Emerging 'Industrial Jurisprudence'" (unpublished Ph.D. dissertation, University of Southern California, 1948), chap. iii.

The above, of course, is a limited view of the effects of discharge. It implies that employees are unaware of the future consequences of their acts and of what happens to other employees who are dismissed.

[29] Together with the less tangible but nevertheless real factors of giving up friends and associates in the shop and in the union; the general depression induced by failure and dismissal; difficulties of job-hunting arising from a bad previous record; and the strain of readjustment to a new and different working environment.

social as well as a personal calamity. It has been the general tenor of decision that the justification for such a calamity should be strictly established before it is permitted. Said one arbitrator, "[J]ustice as well as sound labor relations calls for a degree of proof that is correlative with the high degree of the severity of the charges and penalty imposed. . . ." [30]

Discharge is therefore a frequent subject of grievance and a form of grievance frequently carried to arbitration. As a simple matter of statistics, a discharge appealed to arbitration appears to stand a better than even chance of being reversed in whole or in part. An early study at Rensselaer Polytechnic Institute of 170 arbitration awards in disputes over discharge that were decided during 1946–47 showed management's action sustained in only 34 per cent of the cases as against 64 per cent revoked or modified.[31] This is supported by a comprehensive analysis of the disposition of 1,055 discharge grievances reported in the first 25 volumes of *Labor Arbitration Reports*.[32] The results were management's action upheld in 433 (41 per cent) of the cases, and modified or reversed in 622 (59 per cent). The study was divided into two periods: cases decided January, 1942–August, 1951, and cases decided September, 1951–March, 1956. In the later period there was some improvement in management's showing. The 1942–1951 figures were management unheld in 39 per cent of the cases, and modified or reversed in 61 per cent; whereas for 1951–1956 the ratio was upheld 45 per cent, modified or reversed 55 per cent.[33]

There are of course no data on the disposition of discharge griev-

---

[30] *Discharge for Cause*, p. 15.

[31] J. M. Porter, Jr., "The Arbitration of Industrial Disputes Arising from Disciplinary Action," *Proceedings of the Second Annual Meeting of the Industrial Relations Research Association*, 1949 (1950), pp. 262–263.

[32] J. Fred Holly, "Considerations in Discharge Cases," *Monthly Labor Review*, 80 (June, 1956), 684–688.

[33] Neither of the above are full-count censuses for the periods designated, by whatever standards one might define: by type of dispute, by industry, region, or other. The *Labor Arbitration Reports* consist of selections from decisions submitted by arbitrators. How the selections are made or what per cent they are of the total received is unknown. Some arbitrators do not submit decisions and some of the most important umpire systems (e.g., General Motors) are not represented in the reporting services. However, they are the best data available, and there is some significance in the consistency with which discharges are commuted (in whole or in part) more often than upheld.

ances in the steps before arbitration. Presumably the decisions of arbitrators, with their reasoning, influence both management in its subsequent use of discharge and the parties in their processing of complaints. If this influence is correlative to the decisions (and if the theory of "corrective discipline" is valid), the number of dismissals must have decreased sharply, with suspensions and reprimands substituted therefor to a considerable extent.

Arbitrators' decisions in discharge cases are grounded on a limited number of fundamental concepts. Except as restrained by law or contract, the employer's right to discharge at any time, for any reason or no reason, is absolute.[34] In labor agreements, almost without exception, this right is curtailed, at least to offenses that provide justifiable cause. Even where the agreement is silent on the subject, it has been held that the employer is nonetheless limited to proper grounds in imposing penalties: "The chairman . . . believes a 'just cause' basis for consideration of disciplinary action is, absent a clear proviso to the contrary, implied in a modern collective bargaining agreement."[35] Proper grounds for dismissal, however, may range from the violation of a safety rule to sabotage and theft. The main elements in each decision consist of the terms of the contract, past practice in the firm or plant, and the circumstances of the case.

TERMS OF THE CONTRACT. The terms of agreements with respect to discharge are becoming more specific and more detailed, especially in matters of required procedure: prior notice to, or consultation with, the union, suspension before termination, full and complete statement of charges, union representation at the time of dismissals or before leaving plant, rights of appeal, and accelerated handling of hearings. On the substantive side there is less reliance on "cause" alone as grounds for firing, with the addition of lists of offenses—perhaps separated into classes—the more serious of which may be the basis for summary dis-

---

[34] "Under the traditional business pattern in America, employment is a prerogative of management, to be exercised with an uncontrolled discretion in the absence of statutory or contractual limitation." Arbitrator Maurice H. Merrill, in *American Iron and Machine Works Co. and Intl. Assn. of Machinists* (1952), 5 ALAA 69,134.

[35] Walter E. Boles, Jr., Chairman of Board of Arbitration, in *Cameron Iron Works, Inc., and Intl. Assn. of Machinists* (1955), 25 LA 295.

missal whereas for minor misdemeanors there are intermediate steps of warning and suspension. Employees unjustly terminated are guaranteed reinstatement, back pay, restoration of seniority, and other privileges.[36]

PAST PRACTICE. Where the agreement is silent, either as to specific cause or procedure—as is still the case in many collective bargaining situations—"practice in the plant" is the most influential test. This means simply the customary way of dealing with given classes of rule violations and covers both methods of handling and the relationship of penalties to offenses. A practice employed without dispute over a period of time—say, summary discharge for violation of a "no smoking" rule—has the authority of tradition to support it.[37] A misdeed must be clearly distinguished from previous cases if management wishes to change the penalty or the union to challenge it.

It is also pertinent to recognize the influence of differences in industrial background. . . . How grave a transgression must be if it is to justify discharge depends to some extent on the weight which that penalty is considered to have. . . . The import of discharge is likely to vary from industry to industry. . . . A bank cashier who takes home a few pennies may merit discharge, although a candy maker who eats some bon-bons of equivalent value may not. A musician or actor may be more subject to an unchallengeable management verdict of competence than is a punch-press operator. Discipline—immediate obedience to orders—is more important on a ship than it is in a dress shop.[38]

One advantage of custom as a standard in deciding cases lies in its implication of acceptance by the parties. Another, however, stems from the smoothness and flexibility inherent in its informal character and its allowance for mitigating circumstances. As part of the "common law" of industrial jurisprudence, it permits adjustment to the infinite variations of disputes arising out of daily work patterns. Where the parties trust each other and work

---

[36] See above, chap. ii, for a more complete discussion of this topic.

[37] Arbitrator Frank Wallace Naggi, in *Standard Oil Co. of Indiana and Central States Petroleum Union* (1952), 5 ALAA 69,180. Here the arbitrator upheld the discharge of two men for smoking, on grounds that the penalty was well established in practice and arbitration for both the industry and the refinery where the incidents occurred.

[38] *Discharge for Cause,* p. v.

routines are relatively stable, such informality has much to commend it.

As a practical matter, however, it also has definite weaknesses. In the large plant, with rapid changes of technology and work organization, the likelihood of disagreement between management and employees is increased. Bureaucracy is a function of size, and managerial short cuts[39] based on past practice tend to be regarded with suspicion. In the nature of things, usage provides an uncertain background for either appeal or defense. It is therefore increasingly replaced by contract terminology which defines the rights of employees, union, and management in disputes over termination.[40]

CIRCUMSTANCES OF THE CASE. The most important set of employee defenses against dismissal, however, cannot be put into the agreement because of their innate variety and complexity. These are "mitigating circumstances." It is circumstances that differentiate cases; no two sets of facts are ever identical. And under a theory of "corrective discipline," extenuating circumstances abound. The most prevalent of mitigating factors concern the employee charged with an offense; the longer his service record, the fewer his past rule violations, the more convincing his attitude of honesty and contrition, the weaker the case against him no matter how clearly it falls within the area of proscribed conduct.

Arbitrators are of course not the only people who embrace the philosophy of another chance for the good citizen who has gone wrong, but their inclinations in that direction are clear and unmistakable. These predispositions are supported by an almost unlimited number of possibilities of "contributory negligence" by supervision and fellow employees. Although seldom so stated as a principle, management is clearly expected to show "clean hands" when it closes out a service record. Was supervision careless,

---

[39] Examples might be: substitution of oral for written notice of discharge, bypassing of steps in the grievance procedure, and so on.

[40] Some of the most difficult decisions that arbitrators are called upon to make grow out of clear conflicts between past practice and specifications in the agreement.

faulty, lacking, discriminatory? If so, the benefit of a doubt is raised in the employee's favor. Was the employee heckled or interfered with by other workers? Were tools and materials inadequate in quality or quantity? A whole series of additional problems is raised by the necessary accommodation of managerial authority to the dual role of the union representative in the plant, at times a subordinate and at other times an equal and perhaps an adversary.

The manner and timing of disciplinary action, particularly discharge, presents many opportunities for mitigating circumstances. Advance warnings, promptness of action after the offense is disclosed, consistency of application, access to union representation, written notification, even the question of courteous treatment by supervision and labor relations managers comes up for review. A simple lack of diligence by the company in discovering such a serious misdeed as deliberate falsification may invalidate a discharge. The rule was stated by Harry Shulman in a leading decision in 1945. The facts were not in dispute. An employee rehired after discharge had stated on his second application that he had never been an employee of the company. Said Shulman:

> It can hardly be doubted that such falsification of a material fact . . . is a proper ground for discharge. . . . The question remains, however, of how long an employee's false statement in securing employment can continue to hang over him. . . . Is he subject to discharge for time without limit so long as he remains in the employ of the Company? That would surely be a harsh and unjust rule. . . . In law and morals generally, the principle of a statute of limitations is well recognized, even though it means that the mere lapse of time thus enables a guilty person to escape what otherwise would be regarded as just punishment. The principle is recognized not merely in order to encourage diligence on the part of the aggrieved persons and to direct energies to the relative present rather than to the remote past, but also as a measure of justice to the guilty person whose offense, it is believed, should not render him permanently insecure. . . . The time should be long enough to give the Company ample opportunity in which to learn of the falsification. It should not be so long as to become unjust to the employee. One year is a reasonable period which answers both these requirements. . . . J made his false statement and was hired at Lincoln on August 24, 1943. He was discharged on January 1, 1945. For the reasons stated above, my award is that he be

reinstated without loss of seniority. . . . an award of back pay would be entirely inappropriate.[41]

A key factor in grievance dispositions is the knowledge of the parties that they must continue in a coöperative relationship. As Gollub puts it: "Consistent with the terms of the contract, an [arbitrator's] award may be based in part on an appraisal as to whether and how the human beings involved can be assisted to harmonious future relations." [42] What this means is that the prime consideration in the adjustment of a dispute is a settlement that works, whether or not it squares precisely with the language of the agreement. A labor contract is a static thing; an operating situation a fluid one. Few agreements have been signed that did not at some time or other come up against situations that were neither anticipated nor provided for. Accommodation and compromise are the essence of harmonious relations, and preëminently so in disciplinary matters, where a full catalog of possible infractions and remedies would produce a small encyclopedia. In disciplinary matters, as in industrial relations generally, the pragmatic test must be satisfied. The contract is a means to this end, not an end in itself.

Reduction or cancellation of seniority.—The key factor in the security of the industrial employee is his seniority rights, everywhere protected by contract. In contrast to some other sections of the agreement—for example, discipline and discharge provisions—they are explicitly set forth with all refinements of technicality and detail. Seniority rights are a definite pattern; they establish the position of the employee relative to other workers in cases of layoff, rehiring, promotion, demotion, and transfer. As such, they ordinarily may not be tampered with for disciplinary purposes. However, they are now and then modified or canceled by arbitrators as a substitute form of penalty. A discharged employee may be reinstated with seniority to date from reinstatement, or a part of his seniority (departmental, occupational) may be reduced by a stated amount. The latter action would set the

---

[41] *Ford Motor Co. and UAW*, Opinion A-184 (1945), cited in Shulman and Chamberlain, *Cases*, pp. 466–468. The principle (of a statute of limitations) has now been written into some agreements. See above, chap. ii.
[42] *Discharge for Cause*, p. vi.

employee back in the promotion-demotion sequence, though leaving his layoff and rehiring rights unimpaired.[43]

Required resignation from union office.—This penalty is of course reserved for union representatives who have misbehaved under protection of their positions as stewards, committeemen, and the like. Since the employer is forbidden by law to discriminate against employees on grounds of union membership or activity or to interfere in the selection of representatives for purposes of collective bargaining, the disciplining of union officials is a delicate and difficult job. Unless the misconduct justifies discharge, the man may remain in office though obviously unfitted by temperament and training for his duties. In such circumstances, arbitrators have enforced resignation from office for a period of time as an appropriate remedy.[44] Not all arbitrators would agree, however, that they have the power to remove a union official from office as a disciplinary measure. It has been argued that this constitutes interference with the internal affairs of the union and that the arbitrator may discipline an individual only as an employee and not as a union officer.

---

[43] See, for example, *International Harvester Co. and UAW* (1952), 5 ALAA 69,058, Arbitrator Ray Forrester; *Chrysler Corp. and UAW* (1952), 5 ALAA 69,096, Umpire David A. Wolff, and cases cited later.

[44] See, for example, *Sinclair Refining Co. and OWIU* (1947), 6 LA 965, Arbitrator Dudley E. Whiting; *Johnson-Stephens and Shinkle Shoe Co. and Boot and Shoe Workers of America* (1947), 7 LA 422, Arbitrator Joseph M. Klamon; *International Shoe Co. and United Shoe Workers of America* (1947), 8 LA 746, Arbitrator Maxwell Copelof.

Chapter IV | *Grounds for*
Discipline:
Incompetence and
Negligence

General

In industry, the right to administer discipline and to discharge has always been regarded as a managerial prerogative—a power or privilege associated with office. Before unionization, this power was practically unlimited. It has been one of the major purposes of organized labor to limit managerial prerogative in this area to the exercise of responsible authority under the generally recognized rules of fair play. In recent years, the unions have been notably successful.

Oddly enough, the employers (perhaps unsuspectingly) helped in thus handicapping themselves in the years immediately following World War II by widespread insistence upon a statement of managerial rights in labor agreements. A typical "management prerogatives" clause is as follows:

The right to hire, classify, transfer, promote and demote employees, discharge or discipline employees *for cause*, to maintain discipline and efficiency of employees, to make temporary work assignments and to assign overtime to employees is the sole right of the Company except as limited by the terms of this Agreement.[1]

The key words are "for cause," or, as they have been varied by the preferences of negotiators, "for just cause," "for proper cause,"

---

[1] Commerce Clearing House, *Clauses*, p. 623. (Italics mine.)

"for reasonable cause," "for justifiable cause." In thousands of agreements across the country, these brief phrases have wiped out management's exclusive privileges and immunities and substituted therefor the mandate of due process.

What is "cause"?[2] It is not "any reason or no reason"; it is "good" reason. It implies at a minimum that there must be substantial provable grounds for any action that prejudices the employee's position in the company. An additional implication, according to an overwhelming majority of arbitrators, is that the penalty should be appropriate to the crime.

Any disciplinary action against an employee which is unjust, arbitrary, capricious, or which fails to possess some reasonable foundation for its support, is discipline without "proper cause." Moreover, discipline not amounting to arbitrary or capricious action also lacks cause if the penalty which the Company has imposed bears no reasonable relationship to the degree of the alleged offense.[3]

No legal interpretation is without its dissent, and many arbitrators are lawyers. It would be inconceivable that a term so general and so vital to the interests of both management and employees would be uniformly applied. Since "cause" is the starting point of all employee rights in discipline and discharge cases, what it means has therefore been the subject of considerable debate. The outcome has been two schools of thought, the first—and dominant—point of view being for a broad definition, whereas the second favors restriction. According to the first, the essential elements are:

1. That the employee was guilty of the charge—that he committed the offense complained of;
2. That punishment was warranted under the circumstances; and
3. That the degree of punishment imposed—say discharge—was just and proper, for example, that the "penalty fitted the crime."[4]

This is the position of most arbitrators and of organized em-

---

[2] The addition of "just, proper, reasonable," means little, since their opposites are absurd. "Cause" alone is sufficient and is relied upon in a great many contracts.

[3] Arbitrator Gerald A. Barrett in *Lincoln Industries, Inc., and United Furniture Workers of America* (1952), 5 ALAA 69,158.

[4] See "Arbitration under the Labor Contract—Its Nature, Function and Use," in R. E. Mathews, editor, *Labor Relations and the Law* (Boston: Little, Brown, 1953), pp. 536–537.

ployees everywhere, but it is not the view of everyone. Managements generally and a minority of arbitrators subscribe to the doctrine that:

> the arbitrator does not have the authority to substitute his judgment, as to the degree of penalty imposed, for that of management. They say that under the typical discharge clause cited above ["just cause"], only the first two criteria—whether the wrong was committed and whether punishment was warranted—are the only relevant subjects of inquiry. . . .
> The nature of the punishment, or the degree of the penalty, they say, is not part of "just cause," under the contract. Thus, it is contended, if the arbitrator finds that the employee committed the wrong complained of, and he was disciplined for that wrong, the action of management must be sustained, whatever the penalty was. Neither the union nor the employee can then be heard to complain.[5]

In this controversy, the decision has gone against management. The conclusions of authorities, as well as the most cursory examination of discipline and discharge cases, reveal that, barring an explicit prohibition in the contract or in the arbitration submission, arbitrators almost inevitably include the degree of penalty imposed in their tests for "cause."[6] The basis for this attitude has been explained a great many times, but seldom more succinctly than by William M. Hepburn, chairman of a board of arbitration, as follows:

> In order to test the principle [of the Board's authority to modify the penalty], let us suppose a somewhat different case. An employee of many years' standing with a perfect record in all respects is guilty of a minor delinquency. Disciplinary action is justified. He is discharged. The matter is taken to arbitration, and the question . . . is, whether the discharge was "for just cause."

---

[5] *Ibid.*

[6] See Harry H. Platt, "The Arbitration Process in the Settlement of Labor Disputes," *Journal of the American Judicature Society*, August, 1947, pp. 54–60: "Reasonableness of Penalties. In many disciplinary cases, the reasonableness of the penalty imposed on an employee . . . is the question the arbitrator must decide. This is not so under contracts or submission agreements which expressly prohibit [it] . . . but most labor agreements do not contain such limiting clause. In discipline cases, generally, therefore, most arbitrators exercise the right to change or modify a penalty if it is found to be improper or too severe . . . This right is deemed to be inherent in the arbitrator's power to decide the sufficiency of the cause . . . and in his authority to finally settle and adjust the dispute before him."

It seems to me that there are two respects in which a discharge may be said to be not for just cause. If the facts . . . are not true. . . . And if the facts are true, but the penalty of discharge is out of proportion to the offense. . . . That there may be just cause for disciplinary action does not mean that there is just cause for particular disciplinary action. We do not hang a man for a traffic violation, and a Board of Arbitration . . . has the duty, to evaluate the propriety of the penalty in the light of the seriousness of the offense.[7]

There are of course many "good" reasons for discipline in all its forms up to and including discharge. These, however, are no longer the exclusive property of the employer; they must submit to public scrutiny and satisfy the critical examination of union representatives and impartial judges as to their fairness in light of the circumstances of each case. As explained by one arbitrator:

What constitutes just cause where, as here, the parties have not defined its meaning, is a . . . difficult issue to resolve in general terms. *Certain it is that it is not dependent upon the subjective state of mind of the employer.* That the employer honestly believes that he has just cause, that his motives are above reproach, that he believes that the discharge is patently needed in the interest of the efficient running of his business cannot be dispositive. . . . It follows then that in such cases the employer is obliged to establish to the satisfaction of the arbitrator that the facts impelling the discharge actually occurred.[8]

More and more, "cause" is spelled out in the agreement, in whole or in part.[9] The 1953 BNA report contained the information that 96 per cent of the contracts had discipline and discharge provisions, with the greatest increase noticeable "in clauses spelling out more specific grounds for dismissal." Found in only 60 per cent of a similar collection of agreements in 1950, clauses of this type appeared "in 77 per cent of the BNA's current sample."

---

[7] *E. I. du Pont de Nemours and Textile Workers Union* (1947), 9 LA 345. In one of his earliest decisions as Umpire for the Ford Motor Company and the UAW, Harry Shulman addressed himself to the problem, and expounded a philosophy that has guided many arbitrators since. See Opinion A-2 (1943), reported in Shulman and Chamberlain, *Cases*, pp. 524–525.

[8] *Sanford H. Kadish* in *Uinta Oil Refining Co. and Oil Workers International Union* (1952), 5 ALAA 69,204. (Italics mine.)

[9] A minor contribution to the importance of "cause" was the provision in Sec. 10(c) of Title I of the Labor-Management Relations (Taft-Hartley) Act, that the National Labor Relations Board may not order the reinstatement of any individual as an employee who has been suspended or discharged, or the payment to him of any back pay, if the suspension or discharge was for cause.

Other and more specific definitions accompanied the "just cause" provision in by far the majority of the cases; in fact, "only 8 per cent of the contracts" carried this as the only provision dealing with grounds for discharge.[10]

Violation of company rules is a commonly stated justification, with or without inclusion of the rules themselves in the contract. When included, these may be brief and general or numerous and detailed. They may be accompanied by a statement of company responsibility for posting and distribution to employees, and/or made subject to mutual agreement by the union. Where specific grounds for penalties are listed, the clause is often open-end, as follows:

"Cause" shall include, *but shall not be limited to,* a material false statement in an employee's employment application, violation by an employee of a safety rule, continued inability of an employee to meet production standards, failure of an employee to perform his duties to the best of his ability. . . .[11]

Common topics of special condemnation are: absenteeism, tardiness, intoxication, dishonesty, poor work, violation of the agreement, and insubordination. When union security clauses make employee membership compulsory, the company may put the burden of responsibility on the union for discharges made at the latter's request. There is a wide variety of explicit restrictions and permissions relative to some form of union activity (solicitation of membership or dues during working hours or on company property, serving on committees, refusal to cross picket lines, union service outside of hours, etc.). The right to discharge probationary employees without recourse by the employee or the union is often affirmed.[12]

Types of Employee Shortcomings

Discipline and discharge are the penalties imposed by management for employee shortcomings. There are three primary cate-

---

[10] *Union Labor Report* (Washington: Bureau of National Affairs, October 16, 1953), pt. 2.

[11] Commerce Clearing House, *Clauses,* p. 530. (Italics mine.)

[12] This privilege has its limitations. Where there are statutory protections of the right to organize or of nondiscrimination, probationary employees are covered equally in these respects with those on the seniority list.

gories of employee dereliction which are considered grounds for corrective action:

1. Incompetence or negligence: failure to do one's job properly.

2. Personal misconduct: violation of the rules of good behavior, which implies some form of delinquency in manners, morals, or character.

3. Violation of the agreement.

The first two are individual faults, the last primarily a collective matter.[13] These categories in turn may be broken down into a limited number of important subclasses, which are distinguishable in substance and often in treatment. These distinctions are clearly indicated in the opinions of arbitrators (as, for example, in the case of appropriate penalties) and are beginning to be observed in the agreements themselves.

There are 630 arbitration awards dealing with discipline and discharge cases to be found in the first ten volumes of the Bureau of National Affairs' *Labor Arbitration Reports.* On the basis of

---

[13] This classification differs slightly from that of other writers on grievance handling and arbitration. In both J. M. Porter, Jr.'s, article on "The Arbitration of Industrial Disputes Arising from Disciplinary Action," in the *Proceedings of the Second Annual Meeting of the Industrial Relations Research Association, 1949* (1950), and in Van Dusen Kennedy's chapter on "Grievance Negotiation," in Arthur Kornhauser, Robert Dubin, and Arthur M. Ross, editors, *Industrial Conflict* (New York: McGraw-Hill, 1954), "personal misconduct" is divided into two categories: "violation of shop rules" and "insubordination."

The difficulty with this arrangement is that insubordination is practically always a violation of one or more shop rules, and there are always some types of misbehavior appearing that are not covered by the rules. The classification is therefore neither complete nor logical, in terms of the essential character of employee delinquency. The real basis for this four-way division is statistical. It divides disciplinary cases up into four fairly equal categories, since insubordination is the most prevalent form of misconduct (personal). In Porter's note, the breakdown of 197 arbitration awards was:

Misconduct	Per cent
Incompetence	21
Violation of shop rules	30
Insubordination	28
Violation of agreement	21

The Bethlehem Steel report on arbitration classified "Discipline and Discharge" disputes as follows: (1) improper work performance; (2) improper job attitudes (violation of safety rules, insubordination, absenteeism, etc.); (3) improper personal conduct (fighting, abusive language, etc.); and (4) union activity in violation of the agreement.

TABLE 3

GROUNDS FOR DISCIPLINE: DISTRIBUTION OF ARBITRATION AWARDS IN DISCIPLINE AND
DISCHARGE CASES BY EMPLOYER'S CHARGES

Alleged grounds	Awards		
		Number	Per cent
Incompetence or negligence.....................		129	20
Personal misconduct...........................		389	62
Unreliability: tardiness, absenteeism, etc.........	127		
Troublemaking: fighting, etc...................	50		
Endangering safety of self or others............	9		
Insubordination..............................	152		
Dishonesty or disloyalty......................	28		
Immoral, illegal, subversive acts...............	23		
Violation of the agreement......................		112	18
Striking or instigating strike or slowdown........	68		
Improper acts of union reps. (or management)....	44		
Grand total...................................		630	

SOURCE: *Labor Arbitration Reports*, Volumes 1–10, Bureau of National Affairs.

the employers' charges, the distribution among primary categories
and the principal subclassifications is indicated in table 3.[14]

The primary categories.—The major groupings are incompe-

---

[14] This recapitulation involves a considerable redistribution of the classification
used by the BNA in *Labor Arbitration Reports*. The latter has 15 categories, as
follows:

In general (a selection of awards from the other categories, and therefore a duplication..	(75)
Absence from work; absenteeism....................................	64
Altercation with other employees, intimidation, troublemaking, etc........	43
Damage to or loss of machines or materials..........................	13
Dishonesty, theft, or disloyalty....................................	26
Gambling	3
Incompetence or negligence.......................................	116
Insubordination	75
Intoxication	14
Loafing, leaving post, etc...	42
Plant rules violated (ranging from "negligence" to "theft")..............	51
Pressure from union (actually, 2 of 3 were "troublemaking")..............	3
Refusal to accept job assignment or work overtime.....................	69
Striking or instigating strike.......................................	68
Union activities...	43

Total (omitting "in general")   630

tence, personal misconduct in its various forms, and violation of the agreement. Incompetence and personal misconduct tend to shade off into each other where job failure occurs as a result of negligence, but in the main they are distinguishable. Violation of the agreement is also a form of misconduct of the most serious kind, and the penalties are assessed against individual workers, but the essence of the indiscretion is collective action—with or without encouragement of the union—or else misuse of authority by representatives of the union.[15]

There is an important difference between incompetence on the one hand and misconduct, either personal or collective, on the other. Incompetence is morally neutral; misconduct is morally objectionable.[16] The former is a limited fault and often easily curable, by training, transfer, or the like, whereas the latter points to failings much more deep-seated, the eradication of which is difficult and questionable. Incompetence is related to a particular job or class of jobs. A man may be pleasant, honest, sincere, loyal, hardworking, and reliable, and still be incompetent. The work is just beyond him. As a result, he may be transferred, demoted, or even discharged with less stigma than the rebel, the drunkard, or the chronic absentee. The area of fault is circumscribed, being limited to his inability to do certain specified tasks.

This is not true of misconduct, where the great majority of lapses are regarded as evidence of want of character in major or minor degree. At a minimum, they are violations of plant rules such as no smoking or staying within prescribed work limits, and thus point to irresponsibility, whereas at the upper limit they are clear evidence of lack of principle. Unrelated to a particular job, they are by implication transferable and may show up again anywhere in the plant.

In personnel management, the difference in attitude reflects itself in a difference of treatment in the two cases. The incompe-

---

[15] In a few instances, where the union's charge is upheld that management disciplinary action against union representatives is inspired by antiunion prejudice, the case is classed as a violation of the agreement—this time in reverse, by management.

[16] Discharge for incompetence is frequently called "nondisciplinary" discharge, to distinguish it from dismissal for misconduct. This is the explanation of the frequent use of the double term "discipline and discharge," rather than subsuming dismissal under the general term "discipline."

tent employee is more and more regarded as a worker out of place. He is trained, transferred, resettled, rather than dismissed. Since the evidence of inefficiency is more impersonal, being related to standards of output, feelings run less high and the problem can often be worked out acceptably to management, employee, and the union.

It should not be concluded, however, that the ability to perform a job properly is a matter of unconcern either to the company or to the worker. In any activity as competitive as American industry, efficiency is a key test. Management is constantly concerned with quantity and quality of output, and there is no need to labor the point that standards are high. For the employee, likewise, a record of unsatisfactory work performance is a black mark, a handicap to promotion, more desirable jobs, and better pay. Judgments of incompetence are therefore often questioned, both as to accuracy and proper disposition. When the penalty is dismissal, it is resisted strenuously.

Incompetence

Incompetence means that the employee is either unable to do the job he is assigned to—whether from lack of physical ability, of experience, or of skill—or if capable, that he has failed to because of inadequate motivation or some other reason. Whatever the test (quantity, quality, accuracy, regularity), it is job performance that is in question and not the manners or morals of the employee. A deficiency in the latter may affect job performance of course (intoxication, for instance, reduces skill), but the effect upon output is secondary and in many cases need not even be proved.[17] Incompetence, on the other hand, will not stand alone. It is job-connected, and the proof is evidence of negligence or inefficiency in the discharge of duties.

Although the right to judge capability ranks high among managerial prerogatives, the evidence should be tangible and explicit:

---

[17] Many plant rules—e.g., the wearing of badges—and a number of the so-called "grave offenses" (theft, false statements, conviction of penal offense outside the plant, etc.) have no direct connection with the individual's working efficiency, although most of them have some direct or indirect relationship to the success of the organization as a whole.

The evidence submitted by the employer to show that Mike Gamm was, and is, a poor workman is not convincing. No work records were submitted, nor was there any definite evidence of inferior quality or quantity of work during any specific period of time. There was no comparison of the quality and quantity of Mike Gamm's work with that of any other workman or with any standard of work, no evidence of damaging tools or equipment or wasting materials or of injury to any person because of faulty work habits over a period of seven years.[18]

It is only during the probationary period that the employee may be dismissed without assignable reason.[19] Once he goes on the seniority list, he comes within the protection of the "for cause" clause.

The evidence in cases of alleged incompetence is at times complicated and indirect. What is really in question is the employee's qualifications for the job, but these can be determined only by a check of his performance, usually over a period of time.

It is entirely consistent with the determination of proper cause that an employee may be found by trial of substantial duration to be unsuited for particular employment or unreliable or in some other way an unsatisfactory worker. The fact that the conclusion is reached only after extended trial and on the basis of numerous details independently insufficient is not enough to preclude the exercise of fair judgment.[20]

---

[18] Earl J. Miller, Chairman of Board of Arbitration, in *Bauman Brothers Furniture Manufacturing Co. and United Furniture Workers of America* (1948), 10 LA 79.

[19] Even during probation, the employee may have some protection against arbitrary discharge. It depends upon the agreement. A clause reading "The Company reserves the right to discharge or suspend *any* employee for a good and sufficient reason" (italics added) was held to apply to probationary workers, and two laborers first suspended and then discharged on the 179th day of a 180-day probationary period were held to have been dismissed to avoid attainment of seniority and were granted reinstatement with back pay. Arbitrator E. E. Hale in *American Republics Corp. and Oil Workers International Union* (1952), 5 ALAA 69,018.

In all respects other than discharge, the probationary employee under a labor agreement has the same protection as other workers, unless the contract explicitly provides otherwise. The union is his representative, and the employer is not at liberty to take him on at terms or conditions other than those in the agreement. See *Discharge for Cause*, by Myron Gollub, New York State Department of Labor, Division of Research and Statistics (New York: 1948), p. 27.

[20] Arthur R. Lewis, Chairman of Board of Arbitration, in *Bakelite Corp. and Chemical and Crafts Union* (1945), 1 LA 227.

However, job performance is not always clear-cut or measurable. Many jobs have no measurable outputs, and estimates of performance must be based upon other standards: total sales, accident records, absence of complaints from customers, and especially the conclusions of supervisors as to skill, effort, initiative, judgment, and similar matters of a highly subjective nature. Either the weight to be given a particular trait or the accuracy of a supervisor's rating of it may be contested.

A study of 129 arbitrator's awards in cases involving incompetence or negligence, appearing in volumes 1–10 of *Labor Arbitration Reports*, discloses that the most frequent reason offered for reversing or modifying the penalty is inadequate or conflicting evidence. An example is the dismissal of a Class I carpenter for incompetence. The chairman of the Board of Arbitration ruled as follows:

> The chairman, after a careful review of the evidence, is of the opinion that Thomas Wilkinson is not a first-class carpenter. . . . However, not only was Wilkinson hired as a carpenter, and permitted to remain during the probationary period, he was also given five or six merit increases in addition to the general increase. He was reinstated twice with full seniority after illnesses, and on one of these cases a "quit" was changed to a leave of absence.
>
> The chairman believes that, if Thomas Wilkinson was incompetent, he was incompetent from the date of his hire (April 27, 1943) and was as incompetent at the period of each of his merit increases as he was at the time of his discharge. The chairman further notes that the company has ample rights . . . to reclassify or downgrade employees if it can establish that such reclassification is justified. There was no attempt in this case to use this procedure. . . . The chairman is of the opinion that the discharge of Thomas Wilkinson on July 10, 1946, was not from proper cause. . . . it is ordered that [he be reinstated with one-half back pay].[21]

Proof of incompetence runs into a number of presumptions and extenuating factors, owing to the interrelationship of the job with supervision, materials, and equipment. Next to the vagaries of the evidence, inadequate or improper supervision is the chief reason cited by arbitrators for reversing managerial judgments of inefficiency. The discharge of an employee with a ten-year record

[21] Charles G. Hampton in *Master Electric Co. and United Electrical Radio and Machine Workers* (1946), 5 LA 339.

of service on grounds of lack of skill as a patternmaker is such a case. The man had never completed an apprenticeship nor really made patterns at all, but was classified as patternmaker during World War II in line with the general upgrading which went on at the time. When he later on proved unable to do a pattern-maker's work, he was let go. Said the arbitrator:

> The company is not without some fault in the spoilage of patterns . . . it knew Fuller was not a patternmaker, that he needed much supervision and direction, and its foreman was responsible for checking finished patterns. Yet it entrusted the making of important patterns to him without sufficient guidance for his ability.
>
> In view of the fact that the company retained his services for ten years with such knowledge, it should not have cast him aside on the ground that he did not possess the attributes and qualifications of a skilled patternmaker. . . . It could and should have demoted him to a job requiring less skill.[22]

What is meant by "improper" supervision is illustrated in a decision by Benjamin Aaron concerning a discharge for faulty work at a plant of the Consolidated Vultee Aircraft Corpora-tion.[23] The case, like many others, is complicated. The employee, named Pool, was obviously a difficult and contentious person, whom management might very much like to see the last of. After one reprimand, he wrote to his congressman, telling him that the management of the plant was obviously trying to get rid of the older and more experienced employees, and suggesting that the matter was worth investigating. The letter was officially noticed on the floor of the House of Representatives, which did nothing to make Pool the employee most beloved of his superiors. In fact, it was immediately following this that Pool got the impression that supervision was out to "get him," and his fellow employees testified that members of management said he "would not last long."

The incident upon which the dismissal was based was the de-sign and fabrication of a machine tool, which was held to be worthless and was scrapped after inspection. Pool, a Jig Builder

[22] Dudley E. Whiting in *Jarecki Machine and Tool Co. and UAW* (1946), 3 LA 40.
[23] *Consolidated Vultee Aircraft Corp. and IAM* (1948), 11 LA 7.

"A" by classification, was told by the assistant foreman to do the job in the shortest possible time. To quote the arbitrator.

In this instance, contrary to usual practice, Pool was given no sketch [to work from]; he had to design the tool himself and also had to supervise the routing [another departure from the customary]. In preparing his design, as well as in actually building the tool, Pool received practically no supervision.

His suggestion of a welded construction was overruled to bolted construction (less rigid and less satisfactory); there was no checkup on "normalizing" (heat treating); the possibility of defective work by a machinist assistant was passed over with a "visual inspection" by his foreman and the superintendent; and the tool was sent directly to final inspection in spite of the qualms of Pool himself as to its accuracy and strength. In final inspection, the tool was rejected and it was immediately scrapped, another departure from customary practice.

There were other curious elements in the situation. "They [supervision] also let him work in ignorance of the fact that another man, a tool designer, had been ordered to design the same tool." The other man knew of Pool's assignment, but Pool did not have the reverse information nor any assistance which might have been forthcoming from collaboration.

Was Pool given sufficient assistance or supervision? The evidence on this point is perfectly clear, and the Arbitrator is convinced that Pool did not receive assistance or supervision even approximating what was required under the circumstances. . . . Granting that an "A" Jig Builder is expected to work independently for the most part, it is nevertheless apparent that Pool required, and should have received, at least casual supervision. . . . In the opinion of the Arbitrator, the failure of his superiors to provide it relieved him of the responsibility for the poor workmanship on the tool. . . .

The Arbitrator concludes that Pool was discriminated against and that his discharge was not for proper cause. The Arbitrator rejects as unproved the Union's claim that Pool was deliberately framed by the Company. . . . He finds simply that Pool's supervisors seized a convenient opportunity to procure his discharge, and that in so doing they discriminated against him. Under these circumstances, Pool is entitled to reinstatement with back pay.

It is the function of supervision to help employees in their work: to furnish them with advice and information, see that they get the best available material and equipment, check their work, warn them of errors, and to assume general responsibility for their progress and well-being on the job. They are not expected to trick or mislead the employees under them, to lay traps for them, to try to find reasons for getting rid of them, or to make their work more difficult. In addition, supervisory negligence, confusion, and bad temper have all been cited as extenuating circumstances justifying the reinstatement of employees charged with incompetence. The simple facts are that under a labor agreement, supervision must have "clean hands" and meet a reasonable standard of efficiency. With these satisfied, much will be imputed to it, but they are prerequisites.

Physical disability.—One of the more difficult phases of the question of incompetency has to do with physical disability. When is an employee disabled owing to illness or accident, and what are his and management's rights in the situation? In general, arbitrators have tended to uphold the employer on grounds that management has both the right and the responsibility to assure itself of the physical fitness of its employees. However, the judgment must be based on competent medical opinion and if this is contested by the employee's or the union's doctor, a third-party medical opinion may be resorted to. The applicability of sick-leave provisions and the permanence or the impermanence of the health condition are complicating factors.

For example, a stock clerk was discharged because a bad heart condition prevented him from working the required ten-hour day and performing the occasionally strenuous duties of his job (pushing a hand truck, climbing ladders, etc.). The union grieved, arguing that the employee should be transferred to lighter work or given extended sick leave, for which there was provision in the agreement. The arbitrator dismissed the grievance, holding that the employee's job security did not extend beyond his classification and that sick leave was inapplicable as there were no grounds for expecting recovery from this type of disability. As summed up by the arbitrator:

The Company has every right to protect itself, and Mr. Holmes [the employee], from the results of Mr. Holmes' potential serious injury by terminating his services, particularly where the Company demonstrated such a lengthy previous record of good faith attempt to place Mr. Holmes, where there was no showing by the Union of any proper job on which Mr. Holmes could then or in the foreseeable future be placed, where there was no showing of a contractual right to any such other job, where the medical record is so clear as to Mr. Holmes' incapacity, and where substantial evidence demonstrates poor judgment relative to over-exertion, albeit no lack of sincerity, in Mr. Holmes' case.[24]

When there is a conflict of medical opinion, the case is more difficult. It is often resolved by a medical arbitration to break the deadlock, and if either party declines such a conclusion it is likely to forfeit the case.[25] Pregnancy is another difficult issue, raising questions of the company's right to discharge versus the employee's right to sick leave. The problem is therefore frequently covered in the agreement, as follows: "Any female employee shall be given and shall take six months' leave of absence from work without pay in the event of pregnancy, and her seniority rights in such event shall not be impaired."[26]

Negligence.—Negligence is a narrow category of misdemeanors sandwiched in between incompetence on one side and unreliability or insubordination on the other. It is distinguished from incapacity if the employee has demonstrated the ability to perform adequately, but suffers lapses of attention or application which show up in lowered output, an undue accident record, or

---

[24] Arbitrator John R. Van de Water in *Pacific Airmotive Corp. and IAM* (1953), 5 ALAA 69,343.

[25] See *Ideal Cement Co. and United Cement, Lime, and Gypsum Workers Intl. Union* (1953), 5 ALAA 69, 306, Maurice H. Merrill, Impartial Chairman. Here there was direct conflict of views—two doctors on each side—as to the propriety of reëmploying a man who had been operated on for brain tumor. To resolve the disagreement, "the Company suggested that the question . . . be submitted to a board of physicians, one selected by the Company, one by the Union, and a third chosen by these two." The Union declined, and the arbitrator found for the company, holding that the employee had been given adequate opportunity to meet the claim of disability. "Had this offer been acceded to, there would have been an opportunity for the conflicting views expressed in the medical testimony to have been ironed out in a manner far more well informed than can be afforded by a lay arbitrator faced with a disagreement of the experts. With the utmost regret, I find it necessary to rule that this grievance be denied."

[26] Commerce Clearing House, *Clauses,* p. 253.

otherwise. For example, an employee demoted from Serviceman B to Repairman on account of a bad driving record (four accidents in a year, four other accidents previously) was held properly transferred and his grievance dismissed. The prior classification entailed driving a company car on service calls to customers, whereas the latter involved no driving.[27]

The essence of negligence is failure to exercise the degree of care demanded by the circumstances. If the employee is willfully remiss and lowered output, increase of scrap, or damage to materials or equipment result, the action is in effect insubordination and is commensurately more serious. The difficulty with such a determination is that it calls for a judgment of intent, which often can only be inferred.

When there is no charge of willfulness, both the standard of care established by the employer and the evidence necessary to support the penalty have wide margins of tolerance. As an illustration, a subforeman of Hiram Walker & Sons, Inc., was demoted to the classification of General Help because of an accumulation of shipping errors within one year resulting in a claimed overshipment of 43 cases of liquor. The man had seventeen years of service, seven of them as subforeman. There was no question that the shipments were made on bills initialed by him. However, it was brought out at the hearing that during his shift he cleaned up orders begun by others who had failed to initial their part of the bills, and his protest to the foreman had been fruitless. In addition, the testimony of a handwriting expert cleared him of some of the more serious errors. The arbitrator concluded:

that while the Company clearly has a right to demote or discipline employees who do not perform their work satisfactorily, the Company in this case based its decision to demote this employee in a large part upon errors that have not been substantiated. . . . The Company shall reinstate Loren Johnson to the position of Subforeman and compensate him for the difference in earnings.[28]

Negligence, like incompetence, is job connected. It is therefore peculiarly subject to the defenses of unsatisfactory tools or

[27] Arbitrator Joseph F. Donnelly in *Connecticut Power Co. and International Brotherhood of Electrical Workers* (1952), 5 ALAA 68,962.

[28] Arbitrator Peter M. Kelliher in *Hiram Walker & Sons, Inc., and Local 55, Distillery, Rectifying, and Wine Workers' Intl. Union* (1952), 5 ALAA 68,993.

materials, lack of proper supervision (training, instruction, correction, etc.), adequacy of prior warnings, and the "corrective" approach. In a foundry case, two employees working as a team were charged with 25 spoiled pipes, 18 of which were judged by the inspector as defective because of "cold runs" and 7 because of mold blows. The charge was protested on grounds of the quality of the metal (too cold), about which the employees were critical at the time. They had gone to the superintendent who told them "to go ahead and pour." It was established practice in the plant that employees were not penalized for spoilage when they poured under orders of a supervisor. They were accordingly charged with the 7 pipes defective owing to mold blows (which have nothing to do with quality or temperature of the metal), but reimbursed for the 18 "cold runs." [29]

The record in arbitration.—Published arbitration awards are inconclusive as statistical evidence, since no one knows whether the decisions appearing in print are a representative sample of all awards, and there is even less information on grievance handling up to arbitration. However, the statistical evidence of awards in print is rather conclusive. For "incompetence or negligence," the penalty of discharge appears four times out of five. For the

TABLE 4

PENALTIES ASSIGNED IN INCOMPETENCE AND NEGLIGENCE CASES

Penalties	Cases	
	Number	Per cent
Discharge	106	79
Suspension	16	12
Demotion	9	6
Transfer	1	
Probation	1	
Reprimand	1	3
Compulsory Retirement	1	
Total	135[a]	

SOURCE: *Labor Arbitration Reports*, Volumes 1–10, Bureau of National Affairs.
[a] Total disagrees with the number of awards because of the inclusion of more than one grievance in a single decision.

[29] Arbitrator Abbott Kaplan in *Herco Foundry, Inc., and United Steelworkers of America* (1952), 5 ALAA 69,120.

distribution of punishments in 129 cases, see table 4. Arbitrators, in turn, reverse management in whole or in part more than three times out of five on discharges and suspensions (see table 5). Distributions are not presented in cases involving demotions or other less severe penalties, since very few cases were reported.

TABLE 5

ARBITRATORS' DECISIONS IN INCOMPETENCE AND NEGLIGENCE CASES

Decisions	Cases	
	Number	Per cent
ALL TYPES		
Upheld..............................	49	36
Modified............................	30	22
Reversed............................	56	42
Total.........................	135	
DISCHARGE CASES		
Upheld..............................	39	37
Modified............................	27	25
Reversed............................	40	38
Total.........................	106	
SUSPENSION CASES		
Upheld..............................	5	31
Reversed............................	11	69
Total.........................	16	

SOURCE: *Labor Arbitration Reports*, Volumes 1–10, Bureau of National Affairs.

Between them, inadequate evidence and faulty supervision provided more than half the reasons given for reversal or modification of disciplinary action for incompetence and negligence. The two were cited 47 times out of a total of 86. The complete list, in order of frequency of appearance, is as follows:

It must be repeated that the figures just cited are no proof of anything other than the bad judgment of management in carrying to arbitration these particular cases, which the Bureau of Na-

DISTRIBUTION OF REASONS FOR REVERSAL OR MODIFICATION OF PENALTIES IN
NEGLIGENCE AND INCOMPETENCE CASES

Reasons for reversal	Number of cases
Inadequate or conflicting evidence..	27
Faulty supervision..	20
Penalty too harsh for the offense......................................	9
Seniority of the employee an extenuating factor........................	8
Penalty discriminatory: unequally applied.............................	5
Lack of warning of substandard work...................................	4
Condonation of previous similar offenses...............................	3
Conflict with past practice...	3
Failure to provide written notice, required in contract.................	2
Extension of probationary period.......................................	2
Physical disability unproved or no handicap...........................	2
Demotion conflicts with seniority clause...............................	1
Total..	86

tional Affairs chose to print in its excellent reporting service. I doubt very much that there is any close connection between the distribution of shortcomings charged, penalties assessed, and final judgments thus reported, with the total statistical universe, of which this is such a tiny (and probably biased) sample. It seems likely at least twenty grievances involving inefficiency are solved by the parties themselves for every one coming up to arbitration, and there is no estimating the thousands upon thousands of managerial judgments passing unchallenged by unions and employees, owing to their obvious equity and correct procedure.

Nor should the evidence as presented in these cases be misinterpreted. It implies no protection for incompetent or negligent employees, other than a decent respect for length of service as a counterweight to declining ability or a period of undue carelessness. It *does* imply that a charge of inefficiency should be carefully substantiated before being preferred, and that the employee's failure to perform adequately is a primary responsibility of his supervisors, who should first try to correct his failing and then should consider putting him in a job he can do, at all times keeping him advised of the jeopardy to which he is exposed in falling short of standard. In doing this, management should be consistent, considerate, and precise. Requirements of notice and/or discussion with the union should be observed, and "corrective" penalties preferred, but no clear-cut show of inadequacy should be passed over without remark lest it imply condonation. These amenities observed, management's hands are freed to dispose of the case in an appropriate manner, up to and including discharge.[30]

---

[30] See, for example, the award of Edgar L. Warren in *Cannon Electric and UAW* (1952), 5 ALAA 68,995: "If [the employee's] production had not been at the very lowest level of all the employees doing similar work, if a number of warnings [both oral and written] had not been given, or if there had been some indication that after her most recent warning Miss T had conscientiously tried to improve her work, some lesser form of discipline than discharge might be considered as a corrective measure. . . . It appears . . . that this is not the type of situation where further corrective disciplinary measures would lead to efficient work.

Chapter V

Grounds for
Discipline:
Misconduct

Plant Rules

Employee misconduct embraces all the ordinary forms of bad
behavior, with some additional misdemeanors called forth by an
industrial environment. It ranges from plain bad manners to high
crimes such as violence, theft, and sabotage. The special conditions of industrial employment—size, machinery, close quarters,
timing, and coördination—put a premium on responsibility and
strict obedience to orders. Regimentation is inescapable, and
seemingly trivial departures from prescribed routines (wearing
a badge on the belt instead of the left lapel of coat or shirt, over-
staying of rest pauses, etc.) take on the color of delinquency instead of being dismissed as vagaries of personality.

As individual work units get bigger, the circumstances of industrial processing bring more and more workers into interdependence. The freedom of the individual is correspondingly restricted; regulations increase in number and are more sharply
drawn and more strictly enforced. This tendency, natural enough
without outside stimulus, has been strengthened by the demands
of the grievance procedure and arbitration for definite standards
of conduct and consistency of enforcement. Under such conditions, the opportunities for transgression are plentiful.

The standard basis for a charge of misconduct is violation of a
plant rule. The rules themselves are numerous. A National Indus-

trial Conference Board study, published in 1948,[1] listed "regulations on eighty-nine subjects," ranging from the chewing of gum to falsifying records. A more recent editorial note in *Mill and Factory* probably reflects the current direction of at least some managerial thought on the subject.

A great deal of unnecessary grief and confusion could be avoided if all rules pertaining to employe discipline were clearly stated in black and white. If there is a union contract, that is the place to put them. They should also be included in the employe handbook. In any event, don't leave these rules hanging in the air. Make them known ahead of time. Then everybody knows what to expect.[2]

This advice has by no means been carried out as yet. Labor agreements, particularly, carry few detailed lists of rules, with or without penalties attached.[3] Management's right "to promulgate reasonable plant rules and to discipline employees for violation thereof" is generally held to be implicit in its prerogatives whether defined in the agreement or left open.[4] The right is subject to a number of limitations, however. A rule inconsistent with the agreement is void, whether or not the contract so states, as in the following:

The standard rules and regulations of the company shall continue in full force and effect; and the company shall have the right to amend such rules and regulations and make further rules and regulations, providing such rules and regulations, amendments, and further rules and regulations are not contrary to the terms of this agreement.[5]

Also, rules involving changes in wages, hours, or working conditions covered by the contract are not open to management's uni-

---

[1] Geneva Seybold, *Company Rules—Aids to Teamwork*, Studies in Personnel Policy, No. 95 (New York: National Industrial Conference Board, 1948).

[2] *Mill and Factory*, 58 (January, 1956), 75. A persuasive argument for keeping the rules themselves out of the agreement is the doctrine that "after they have once become the subject of mutual agreements, very specific bargaining and agreement are required to make their modification again exclusively a matter of company decisions and announcements." Frank Elkouri, *How Arbitration Works* (Washington: Bureau of National Affairs, 1952), p. 252, quoting from *Ampco Metal, Inc.*, 3 LA 374.

[3] For an example of rule inclusion, but no price list, see *1956 Agreement Between Fruehauf Trailer Co. and UAW, Local 811* (AFL-CIO).

[4] The quote is from Arbitrator Benjamin Aaron in *Douglas Aircraft Co., Inc., and UAW* (1946), 3 LA 598. See also, Elkouri, *op. cit.*, pp. 251-53.

[5] Commerce Clearing House, *Clauses*, p. 683.

lateral determination. They must be negotiated with the union, if the latter challenges them.

The most exacting restraints, however, are applied to rule administration. Put negatively, the latter may not be "arbitrary, unreasonable, or capricious."

> [The company] cannot follow a policy of ignoring certain infractions of a rule and then, suddenly, enforce the rule to the limit against one employee. Neither can it tacitly forgive rule violations by failing to discipline the offending employee, and then, at a later time, cite those past misdeeds in justification of a discharge ostensibly occasioned by an offense which does not, in itself, warrant such drastic action.[6]

The formal adoption and official posting of rules is increasingly accepted as a prerequisite to their enforcement. Shulman argued this in an early case, as follows:

> The Union protests, in the first place, that no rule against card playing had been published by the Company. At least one of the aggrieved employees, who had been recently transferred to Highland Park from Rouge, testified convincingly that he had no knowledge of such a rule. The Company asserts that "the Union" and many employees had been told a number of times that card playing on Company property was against Company rules. But it is admitted that no rule against card playing had been promulgated in writing and published to the employees by means of rule book or posting on bulletin boards and the like.
>
> Regulation of employees' personal conduct in the plant ought not to be left to haphazard, word of mouth communication. Insofar as possible, a rule prohibiting certain conduct should be promulgated and posted in such a way that no employee can reasonably plead ignorance.[7]

Retroactive liability, owing to a change in the rules, is unfair.[8]

The above are general standards of rule administration. There are variations in the requirements, depending on the type of rule which is violated, or, to put it another way, the nature and seriousness of the misdemeanor charged to the employee.

---

[6] Arbitrator Benjamin Aaron in *Douglas Aircraft Co., Inc., and UAW* (1946), 3 LA 598.

[7] *Ford Motor Co. and United Automobile Workers*, Opinion A-133 (1944), cited in Shulman and Chamberlain, *Cases*, p. 399.

[8] For instance, a rule change making dismissal mandatory upon a third or fourth offense of any kind would automatically clear the records of employees guilty of past violations. They would be permitted to start over.

Employee misconduct falls into six rather distinct classes. The classes are not completely separable (e.g., leaving off gloves and goggles may be grouped under either insubordination or violation of a safety rule), but the general pattern is plain enough. The principal headings, in a rough order of ascending gravity, are as follows:

a. Unreliability: a very broad category, the essence of which is failure to fulfill the time or attention requirements of the job —tardiness, absenteeism, loafing, leaving work station, and so on.

b. Troublemaking: interference with other employees in such a way as to create disorder.

c. Endangering the safety of oneself or others.

d. Insubordination: defiance of the authority vested in management.

e. Dishonesty or disloyalty: theft, falsification of records, disclosure of confidential information.

f. Immoral, illegal, or subversive activity: "grave offenses," objectionable to the moral standards of the community.

Unreliability

Unreliability, like negligence, is a type of misconduct closely related to incompetence and is often cited as evidence of the latter. The thing that distinguishes it is its transferability. Absenteeism, tardiness, and time-wasting are general traits, unconnected with specific occupations.[9] They are also hard to cure. Industrial employment demands regularity of attendance and close attention to the work at hand. Operations are often carefully timed, and the work of one man may be a necessary precedent to that of another or several others. Where jobs are in sequence or coöperative, as on moving assembly lines, failure at one station may delay the work of many. The principal deficiencies of this class are:

1. Habitual tardiness or absenteeism without notice or good cause.

2. Failure to report for overtime work when scheduled.

3. Leaving work station without permission.

---

[9] There are exceptions, of course. Some kinds of jobs present more opportunities than others for specific kinds of inattention. E.g., sleeping on the job is more prevalent on graveyard shifts than in the daytime.

4. Wasting time: loafing, loitering, reading, or sleeping on the job.

5. Receiving visitors or sending and receiving personal mail, telephone calls, and telegrams while at work.

The major characteristics of unreliability as an industrial misdemeanor is its limited impact in the individual case as compared with its upsetting character when widely prevalent or carried to extremes. A single instance of lateness at work, unreported absence, or wandering away from work station is seldom critical. However, chronic lapses of this sort on the part of one employee or a group of employees can introduce an element of uncertainty into operations that may be disastrous. The main problem is administration: where and how to draw the line.[10] The criteria for management to keep in mind are: definite standards of conduct expected of all employees, a schedule of appropriate but specific penalties to be applied in case of breach, and certainty and consistency of enforcement.

Definite standards of conduct.—This means the rules for attendance and attention to work while on the job: what constitutes proper notice or excuse in cases of tardiness or absenteeism; how permission to leave early or be away from the bench temporarily is obtained; prohibited conduct, as reading or sleeping while on duty; under what conditions visitors may be received or phone calls made. Some of the limitations and the accompanying penalties may be found in the agreement—for example, loss of holiday pay for absence the workday preceding or following the holiday, automatic separation and termination of seniority for absence without notice or proper excuse for three or five days.[11] The others should be either covered in detail or included in general rules which are made a part of the contract, published in an employee handbook, or posted on plant bulletin boards.

Schedule of penalties.—If the argument for a "price list" is valid anywhere in the disciplinary procedure, this is the spot for it. Failures of attendance or of attention to the job are by no

[10] See Paul Prasow, "An Examination of the Role of Arbitration Principles in an Emerging 'Industrial Jurisprudence'" (unpublished Ph.D. dissertation, University of Southern California, 1948), for a thorough review of the many problems connected with absenteeism alone.

[11] Commerce Clearing House, *Clauses,* pp. 160, 458.

means uniform in their impact on work processes, but the range
of probable interference is considerably narrower than in matters
of insubordination, troublemaking, theft, and the like. The fault is
usually one of omission rather than commission, and in the typical
case the individual incident is annoying rather than costly. The severity of the penalty may therefore properly be related to the frequency of occurrence within given time periods on a graduated
scale; 1st time, oral warning; 2d time, written reprimand; 3d time,
short suspension; etc. There are other advantages as well. This is
the "corrective" approach; it puts the employee on notice, thus
serving as a warning or series of warnings, and gives him an opportunity to correct his faults. It also tends to standardize the administration of discipline in an area where there are many infractions,
concerning which the attitudes of individual supervisors might
vary considerably.

Certainty and consistency of enforcement.—A foolish consistency may be the hobgoblin of little minds, but a careless inconsistency in the administration of plant discipline will produce
many grievances and prove very costly to management. A standard uniformly applied by arbitrators to disciplinary cases is the
certainty of enforcement, with its counterpart of condonation.
Another measure of discipline is its conformity to other penalties
for similar offenses—for example, consistency. Both of these are
important for cases in which a cumulative record of violations is
cited as justification for the strictness of the punishment.

A rule violation overlooked is very likely to be held an offense
condoned, with the employer estopped from using it later as
grounds for corrective action:

The past practices of any employer in dealing with such matters
as absenteeism and tardiness among its employees may constitute
standards of future behavior by the employer just as surely as if those
standards were embodied in a collective bargaining agreement. . . .
The number of Miss Peabody's absences was probably not excessive.
The tardiness may or may not have been justified; but the employer,
having failed on even one occasion to reprimand Miss Peabody during
the entire previous year, cannot now take the position that these past
tardinesses constitute a sufficient excuse for her summary dismissal.[12]

[12] Benjamin Aaron, Chairman of Board of Arbitration, in *Dist. Lodge No. 727,
IAM, and Office Employees Intl. Union, Local 30* (1947), 7 LA 231.

A series of warnings not subsequently carried out may also imply condonation, even of very serious misdemeanors, and a weakening of the employer's position.

> The evidence shows that during this period, the aggrieved was warned on several occasions concerning his work. . . . participation in a slow-down, absences from his post of duty, failure to maintain certain quality standards, and, finally, falsification of his Piece-Work Reports. . . . The Company exercised patience in dealing with the aggrieved, since discharge would have been justified . . . when he did take part in a slow-down, or . . . falsify a time record, or . . . deliberately refuse to comply with his foreman's instructions. . . . Notwithstanding these previous acts, the Company continued him as an employe. Its position was therefore weakened when it summarily discharged him for acts of a similar nature.[13]

Certainty of enforcement does not necessarily mean rigid application of the letter of the law. A penalty may be waived or modified for a variety of reasons.[14] However, outright disregard of rule violations or the failure to punish offenses following warnings are poor precedents if management intends the rules to be observed.

Condonation is based on the record of the individual employee. It is an internal test of the reliability of the enforcement machinery. Consistency brings in comparisons with the treatment of other employees. What it means is that all employees should be treated alike. A prime illustration of this principle is found in the decision of Gerald A. Barrett, Arbitrator, in *Lincoln Industries, Inc., and United Furniture Workers of America*.[15] Here the president of the local union was first suspended indefinitely and then discharged, primarily on the grounds of fraudulent entries on his time card.

The claimed fraudulent entries all concern the lunch hour period, which runs from 12 noon to 12:45, and during which no pay is

---

[13] Arbitrator Jacob J. Blair, in *Pennsylvania Transformer Co. and USWA* (1952), 5 ALAA 69,209.

[14] See Arbitrator Harold M. Gilden in *John Morrell and Co. and United Packinghouse Workers of America* (1948), 9 LA 931: "Discipline may be amply justified in instances of excessive absences. The determination of the propriety and the reasonableness of the penalty must take into account such factors as seniority, previous warnings directed to improvement in attendance records; the number of absences complained of; the alleged reasons for the absences, and whether or not the employees reported off."

[15] (1952), 5 ALAA 69,158.

granted by the Company. . . . The Company established that many of the entries on Ferguson's time cards were inaccurate for the lunch period . . . that some showed a lunch period of no more than a few minutes when it was admitted that he went home for lunch, and others which showed that he punched out for lunch and back in after lunch at the same time.

The Union conceded these inaccuracies . . . but denied that they constituted any justification for discipline. The Union demonstrated by undisputed evidence that it has been a common practice throughout the plant for employees to punch other employees' cards and to punch out and in at the same time, all with respect to the lunch hour. . . . It is significant that a random sample of 656 cards containing 2,670 punched entries reveals that 1,937 or 72 per cent of the total entries were punched out and in at the same time. . . . of 43 entries on the time cards of assistant foremen, 30 were punched out and in at the same time.

The practice is a violation of a Company rule, but the testimony is overwhelming that the rule has been largely ignored in the past not only by the employees themselves but also by management representatives. The Company may not now discipline an employee for violations of the rule when it has had knowledge of and overlooked consistent violations throughout the plant over a long period. . . . The conclusion is inevitable that Ferguson's discharge is not for "proper cause." . . .

Extenuating circumstances.—When the gravity of the individual offense is slight, the manner in which discipline is administered becomes of primary importance and extenuating factors crop up everywhere. Take absenteeism, for instance. Customarily, advance notice to the employer relieves the employee of blame, or at least limits his responsibility. What is sufficient notice? Is it one or two or twenty-four hours ahead of the shift? Is oral notice sufficient or must it be in writing? What is "constructive" notice? If a telegram is filed eight hours ahead but delivered after the shift opens, has the employee discharged his obligation to the company? Is a request to a fellow employee on a prior shift, relayed to that employee's foreman but then forgotten, sufficient notice? The notice problem works in reverse too. A call back to work by the company (or a notice not to report) must also meet the requirements of timeliness and sufficiency, if failure to report is to be charged against the employee.[16]

---

[16] See Prasow, *op. cit.*, for a discussion of these points.

In every case, of course, the contract between the parties governs, and there is a broad variety of provisions covering proper notice, good cause, and appropriate penalties for failure to check in. Technicalities arise, as in a case where an employee left word for his foreman five hours ahead of the beginning of the shift that he would be absent. When he did report the following day, he refused to explain his absence on grounds that he had satisfied the contract requirement which provided for a three-day suspension if the employee "fails to notify the company when absent from work [by at least 4 hours before the start of the shift]; or fails to give satisfactory reasons for such absences." When it was disclosed that he had asked to be excused to go to a basketball game that evening and had been refused, he was laid off for three days: Said the arbitrator:

> This arbitrator reluctantly finds that Mr. Proehl has complied with the contract as written. The contract does not specifically say that he must notify the company four hours in advance *and* present a reasonable excuse. It specifically says "*or* present a reasonable excuse."
> It is obvious . . . that Mr. Proehl has taken advantage of the wording of the contract. . . .
> Under the facts and circumstances of this case, Mr. Proehl, not having violated the letter of the contract, should not have been given a three-day suspension. Therefore, the company should reimburse Mr. Proehl for the three days.[17]

In-plant absenteeism.—Failure to report on time or at all is one kind of absenteeism. Another is what may be called "in-plant" absenteeism: leaving work station without permission, punching out early, stretching lunch hours or rest periods, loafing, sleeping on the job. In these cases, the propriety of the excuse offered by the employee is foremost, and where the penalty is reasonable, arbitrators will seldom disturb it. For example, 5 employees of the Chrysler Corporation left the plant early in the shift on grounds that it was too cold to work. However, 81 other employees stayed on with no ill effects, and it was established that less than thirty minutes after the five left, the temperature was satisfactory. The 5 argued that the foreman had acquiesced in

---

[17] Arbitrator Walter G. Seinsheimer in *The Mead Corp. and District 50, UMW* (1953), 5 ALAA 69,314.

their leaving, but this was denied and no pass-out slips had been issued. A one-day disciplinary suspension was upheld.[18]

Summary discharge for a single lapse, on the other hand, is an open invitation to reversal or modification. The employee's age, his seniority, his prior record, managerial practices such as lack of warning—any or all may be construed as mitigating circumstances affecting the justness of the cause. For example, an employee with eight years of seniority was found asleep on the job, was photographed by company guards, and was discharged. The man was an asphalt tester, with an otherwise spotless record with the company and a reputation for good citizenship in the community. The company had encouraged employees to take "5 or 10" minute rest periods when work permitted. Said the arbitrator:

> On the evening in question, Mr. Thomas' work was light. There is no positive evidence to the effect that he neglected his work at this or any other time. . . . There is a very narrow line between "take five or ten," and twenty minute "catnapping." . . . the arbitrator feels that the years of seniority and satisfactory service rendered by Mr. Thomas to his Company shows that his punishment was excessive . . . it is [his] decision that P. A. Thomas be reinstated by the Company with full seniority within three days of the date of reception of this award, but that no back pay be awarded. . . .[19]

Penalties.—A succession of minor indiscretions, either alone or combined with other faults, will provide grounds for disciplinary action up to and including discharge, if proper warnings are issued, a "corrective" approach is followed, condonation is absent, and penalties are consistently applied. In one case, an employee had six conduct reports for absenteeism, was suspended for a week after failure to improve his record, and upon return to work was warned that if his attendance fell below plant average for any month he would be discharged. It did so the month following, he was dismissed, and a grievance was filed. The employee claimed illness as the reason for two absences in the final month,

---

[18] Umpire David A. Wolff in *Chrysler Corp. and UAW* (1952), 5 ALAA 69,129.

[19] Arbitrator Jack Johannes in *American Liberty Oil Co. and Oil Workers Intl. Union* (1953), 5 ALAA 69,313.

elimination of which would have brought his record above the plant average. The arbitrator's reasoning was as follows:

> In the approximately 4 years that Christopher was in the employ of the Company, he was absent 140 days and late on 88 other days.
> Were these absences [in the final month] to stand alone or be compared with a record of infrequent absences, they could not possibly have constituted just cause for discharge. This employee had received 6 warnings and a suspension for prior poor attendance. No company can function on any reasonable scheduled basis if employees were to maintain records of attendance such as the one exhibited. . . . Christopher had ample opportunities to improve his record. He failed to do so within the limits set by the company in the last conduct report prior to discharge. Setting a maximum of plant average in this case was certainly a reasonable basis of comparison. Even though Christopher may have had reasons, ordinarily valid, for absences on the two days prior to discharge, they cannot in this instance be excluded from his attendance record. . . . The arbitrator is of the opinion that Christopher was not unjustly treated and the grievance should be denied.[20]

Even minor penalties may be improper, however, if inconsistently applied.[21]

The employer is justified in expecting promptness, regular attendance, and attention to duty while on the job. The primary problem in the enforcement of these requirements is administrative. In the large plant, particularly, there are many opportunities for inconsistency, condonation, and extenuating circumstances. Reasonable rules, uniform enforcement, with penalties increasing in severity as demerits accumulate, is the correct approach to the problem. Discharge for a bad record is justifiable, if the employee is warned of his jeopardy yet persists in rule violation; lesser discipline is seldom disturbed by arbitrators if the facts support the charge.

For what it may be worth, the record of reported arbitrations in unreliability cases shows that discharge outranks lesser penalties two to one, with the punishment being upheld two times out of five and reversed or modified the rest of the time (see tables 6

---

and 7). One-third of the discharges are upheld and slightly more than half of the disciplinary layoffs (see table 7).

The customary *caveat* must be repeated. These statistics are based upon a limited sample of arbitration awards alone. They imply nothing whatever concerning the disposition of grievances by the parties or the distribution of penalties by employers in the total universe of rule infractions for tardiness, absenteeism, and the like. This does not mean, however, that they are without significance. There is sufficient agreement among arbitrators concerning the correct handling of discipline in those cases to make a definite pattern for employers to follow if they choose to heed the warnings. It seems more than likely that this pattern will eventually set the limits for "proper cause" in terms of procedure, grounds for action, and appropriate penalties.

Troublemaking

The essence of troublemaking is interference with other employees on the job. This interrupts work, exacerbates tempers, and produces disharmony. Whether or not the extreme emphasis of recent years on "harmonious in-group relations" is justified, there can be no doubt that the workplace houses a social organization as well as a functional one. As such, the former has one peculiarity; it is a captive group. So long as an employee chooses to work there, his associates must be his fellow workers. He cannot avoid the boor, the practical joker, the profane, the abusive, the quarrelsome. This being the case, plant managements properly attempt to protect the personal privacy of employees as far as possible from unacceptable intrusions. These consist mainly of the following:

1. Fighting or instigating a fight.
2. Threatening, intimidating, or coercing other employees.
3. Horseplay and practical jokes: running, scuffling, throwing things.
4. Vulgar, profane, or obscene language, especially before women.
5. Petty annoyances of various kinds: forcing uninvited opinions on others, loud talking or whistling, playing personal radios, etc.

TABLE 6

PENALTIES ASSIGNED IN UNRELIABILITY CASES

Penalties	Cases	
	Number	Per cent
Discharge..........................	111	68
Suspension.........................	49	38
Warning...........................		
Loss of seniority..................		
Demotion..........................	4	2
Reprimand.........................		
Total..........................	164ᵃ	

SOURCE: *Labor Arbitration Reports*, Volumes 1–10, Bureau of National Affairs.
ᵃ Total disagrees with the number of awards because of inclusion of more than one grievance in a single decision.

TABLE 7

ARBITRATORS' DECISIONS IN UNRELIABILITY CASES

Decisions	Cases	
	Number	Per cent
ALL TYPES		
Upheld............................	65	40
Modified..........................	51	31
Reversed..........................	48	29
Total..........................	164	
DISCHARGE CASES		
Upheld............................	38	34
Modified..........................	45	41
Reversed..........................	28	25
Total..........................	111	
SUSPENSION CASES		
Upheld............................	26	53
Modified..........................	6	12
Reversed..........................	17	35
Total..........................	49	

SOURCE: *Labor Arbitration Reports*, Volumes 1–10, Bureau of National Affairs.

6. Selling, soliciting, or raising contributions, unless authorized.

7. Distributing unapproved written or printed matter in the plant.

The two main difficulties in administering discipline for troublemaking are: getting the facts, and deciding where the individual liberties of employees in matters of self-expression end and infringement of rights of others begins. When the outcome is a fight, there is no doubt of guilt, but there may be considerable doubt as to whose guilt it is. No single simple rule will suffice—neither the first word, the original challenge, nor the first blow. An investigation almost always uncovers a trail of disputes, charges, and recriminations which are quite difficult to untangle. Since fighting is a serious offense, it is often listed in company rules as grounds for summary dismissal. Where the evidence with regard to instigation fails to point clearly to one of the parties, discharge of both is often resorted to.

Fighting.—Fighting is an extreme form of interference with other employees and is the type of dispute in this category most often carried to arbitration. The standard penalty is summary dismissal. Many companies have an established policy of discharging both parties, on the theory that an actual altercation is avoidable if either of the principals is peaceably inclined.[22] The theory is buttressed by the practical difficulty of separating out the aggressor from the aggressee in the mass of conflicting details which always accumulates about a personal encounter. That the difficulty is extreme is clear, both a priori and from reading almost any arbitration award on the subject.

A fair example is found in the decision of G. Allen Dash, Jr. in *Minneapolis-Honeywell Regulator Co. and IUE*.[23] The immediate train of events began with a series of strong protests from one employee to a group of workers around a near-by water cooler against being "showered with paper cups containing water." At the third remonstrance, one of the listeners, who had been present each time a complaint was registered, took offense, issued a

---

[22] This flies in the face of Mr. Dooley's famous dictum that if a man wants to visit with you, drink with you, or play a game of cards with you, you can decline, but if he wants a fight you've got to oblige him.

[23] (1953), 5 ALAA 69,276.

challenge, and the two retired out of sight through a doorway and exchanged blows. Both were discharged and the employee issuing the challenge grieved, claiming lack of responsibility. The arbitrator summarized thusly:

Both parties freely agree that Employee F. R. was the one who initiated the suggestion that the two employees leave the Company premises to "fight out" this situation. Both parties are in full agreement that Employee F. R. led the way out of the work area to a nearby enclosed stairway, and that Employee C. F. followed him. . . . The Company reasons that Employee F. R.'s invitation to Employee C. F. to go outside and Employee C. F.'s acceptance of this challenge represented a clear intention on the part of both of them to fight. . . .

Regardless of whether or not Employee F. R. had anything to do with the throwing of the water containers at Employee C. F., his subsequent actions after the third time Employee C. F. protested his treatment were not those of an innocent bystander. . . . Rather, he was a participant whose degree of guilt is questionable, but who must accept the consequences of his actions.[24]

However, it must be fighting and not assault. In an early case, a union official by the name of Willis, chairman of the bargaining committee, referred to the works manager of the plant as "a damn liar." The works manager had Willis summoned to his office and there attacked him without warning, beating him severely, following which he submitted his resignation and walked out of the plant. When Willis recovered from his injuries and reported back to work he was denied reinstatement on grounds of a " well-established and recognized policy of disciplining all participants in a fight without regard as to who is responsible or who is most at fault." The arbitrator reinstated Willis with full back pay, on the following grounds:

The evidence discloses that several blows were struck at Willis, without any previous warning, while he was standing with his hands in his pockets and even after [he] had fallen into a chair and was unable to defend himself. To characterize this as a "fight" so as to charge Willis with responsibility for it is, I think, to do violence to the English language if not also to the American conception of that fair sport.[25]

---

[24] *Ibid.*
[25] Arbitrator Harry H. Platt in *Palmer-Bee Co. and USWA* (1945), 2 LA 63.

A company applying the joint-responsibility rule must also be careful to avoid any appearance of discrimination. For instance, two employees were discharged for fighting by the Paranite Wire and Cable Corp. in March, 1947. One of them was rehired as a new employee in June. When the other party to the fracas heard of this, he grieved that the action was discrimination and requested reinstatement. The award was that:

> The grievance . . . is granted and [Medler] should be put back to work on the same basis as Stallard McNutt. . . . His seniority rights and his former classification should be disregarded in his reëmployment. These were lost by McNutt, so they should also be lost by Medler. Medler is entitled to back pay from the date McNutt was rehired less his earnings elsewhere during that period. . . .[26]

Although arbitrators in general uphold the joint-responsibility rule where it has been a standard company policy, there are exceptions. An example is the decision of Whitley P. McCoy in *Goodyear Clearwater Mills, Inc. and TWUA*. The facts are as follows: Employee A called Employee B "a tallow-faced s.o.b." B threw a piece of wood at A but missed. A drew a knife and chased B, who ran away, throwing more wood in self-defense. Both men were discharged. The arbitrator upheld the discharge of A for drawing a knife, but reinstated B since his offense "was a simple assault, and did not result in a battery, and . . . there was some provocation for that in the term which had been applied to him. . . ."[27]

For lesser offenses—intimidation, horseplay, disagreeableness— the evidence is often highly circumstantial and degrees of guilt are difficult to assess. The discharge of a female employee of five years seniority for incompatibility, for instance, was based on testimony that "other people could not or would not work with her. . . . Girls so assigned were observed to have been engaged in altercations with her and sometimes were said to have gone weeping to the women's rest room." The work being done re-

---

[26] Arbitrator Edward E. Greene in *Paranite Wire and Cable Corp. and IBEW* (1947), 9 LA 112.

[27] (1947), 8 LA 647. The award is curious, in that B's assault did not result in a battery either. Presumably, the use of an opprobrious term plus resort to a knife added up to more than throwing the piece of wood.

quired group collaboration, and the arbitrator concluded as follows:

> The written statements by some of the union members that Mrs.
> Lahue was well-liked and was friendly to all seem incredible under
> the circumstances. It is diametrically opposed to the usual conduct of
> the employer to discharge an able and efficient employee for no reason.
> . . . The explanation of the discharge given by the employer appears
> to be sustained by the evidence and by reason. In any direct conflict
> of testimony, such as is present here, a person charged with the
> obligation of deciding facts must lean heavily upon collateral, con-
> temporary and corroborative factors. If it were true that Mrs. Lahue
> was pleasant and congenial, as contended by the union, the conduct
> of other women in wanting to quit working in her immediate vicinity
> is unexplainable . . . and the conduct of the company in discharging
> an admittedly able and intelligent employee would be illogical and ab-
> surd. . . . It is therefore concluded that Mrs. Lahue's conduct reg-
> ularly and improperly interfered with production in the area in which
> she was employed.[28]

As in the Minneapolis-Honeywell case above, troublemaking frequently either originates in or takes the form of practical jokes, which are annoying to the butt and may be dangerous as well. In such cases, the jokesmith is usually held subject to discipline if he can be identified. This may be no easy task and arbitrators as well as management are often faced with directly conflicting testimony, withholding of evidence by one or both parties to the case, unwillingness of fellow employees to testify, and other similar difficulties.[29]

Published arbitration awards in troublemaking cases show the penalty to be discharge nine times out of ten, with about the usual proportion of penalties of all types upheld (see tables 8 and 9).

Endangering Safety of Self or Others

If published awards are any criterion, either relatively few violations of safety rules become grievances, or else the settlement

---

[28] Clarence M. Updegraff, Impartial Chairman, in *Turner Co. and IBEW* (1953), 5 ALAA 69,332.

[29] See *Food Machinery and Chemical Corp. and District 50, UMWA* (1952), 5 ALAA 69,082, Sanford H. Bolz, Impartial Chairman, for an extreme example of the difficulty of ascertaining the facts in a horseplay case.

TABLE 8

PENALTIES ASSIGNED IN TROUBLEMAKING CASES

Penalties	Cases	
	Number	Per cent
Discharge........................	50	89
Suspension..	4	7
Transfer.........................	2	4
Total	56ᵃ	

SOURCE: *Labor Arbitration Reports*, Volumes 1–10, Bureau of National Affairs.
ᵃ Total disagrees with the number of awards, because of the inclusion of more than one grievance in a single decision.

TABLE 9

ARBITRATORS' DECISIONS IN TROUBLEMAKING CASES

Decisions	Cases	
	Number	Per cent
ALL TYPES		
Upheld...........................	25	45
Modified	19	34
Reversed.........................	12	21
Total	56	
DISCHARGE CASES		
Upheld...........................	20	40
Modified	19	38
Reversed.........................	11	22
Total	50	

SOURCE: *Labor Arbitration Reports*, Volumes 1–10, Bureau of National Affairs.

rate in prearbitration steps of the procedure is high. Only nine such disputes were reported in the first ten volumes of *Labor Arbitration Reports,* and of these, five were violations of "no smoking" rules.[30] The principal ways in which safety may be endangered are as follows:

---

[30] Volume 5 of *American Labor Arbitration Awards* corroborated this. It contained only one case of safety rule violation, again an infraction of a "no smoking"

1. Violation of safety rules or practices: clothing (gloves, glasses, shoes, etc.), machine guards, load limits, fire doors, etc.

2. Unauthorized possession of weapons or explosives on company property.

3. Smoking, except at designated times and places.

4. Failure to observe traffic regulations.

5. Failure to report an injury or a contagious or communicable disease.

One reason for the low incidence of arbitration awards may be the high standing of safety rules with both employers and employees. In many plants, a poor safety record is an unforgivable sin. The reasons are both humanitarian and practical. The former is obvious; there is danger enough of death or dismemberment from high-speed industrial operations under the best of conditions, and no compensation plan can cover the full cost of suffering and family deprivation. On the practical side are the avoidance of interference with production caused by accidents and the expense of insurance, which varies directly with the accident rate. Insurance companies have been indefatigable in campaigning for safe work practices, and all accident research has pointed to the importance of observing safety rules and regulations.

Another peculiarity of safety rule arbitrations is the low proportion of penalties upheld. Only two of the nine disciplinary actions were affirmed, three were modified, and four reversed.

The grounds for modification or reversal were condonation by the employer (four cases, of which three were violations of "no smoking" regulations), extenuating circumstances, and entrapment. If the employer overlooks rule violations or winks at them, especially if the company is benefited thereby, a clear change of policy with public announcement and warnings is necessary before disciplinary action may be imposed. The following case illustrates this principle. A pitman in a steel plant moved a crane, notwithstanding a rule limiting crane operation to regular opera-

---

rule. The author recognizes of course that this limitation is partly due to the classification system employed. If "horseplay" or "intoxication" were included in the safety category, for example, the number of awards would be doubled or tripled. This is one of the dilemmas of classification, of course, and another classifier might well give a different answer. However, little damage is done if the contents of the different classifications are known and the basis for their selection revealed.

tors. The crane was damaged. The employee was given a disciplinary layoff of five days. The board of arbitration (including the employer's representative) was unanimous in reversing the company, with the following explanation by the chairman:

> The crane has to be moved at times to make way for another crane bringing a ladle. If the first crane is moved by one of the pitmen, the operator of the second crane is saved the trouble and the time of climbing down from his crane, climbing up on the other crane, moving it, then climbing down and up on his own crane again. . . . [Sometimes, when an operator was not around, letting a pitman move the crane saved an hour or more of time.] Caracappa testified that he customarily moved the crane about twice a shift . . . and that other nonoperators did so too.
>
> The arbitrators are unanimous that the penalty of a five-day suspension should not have been imposed in this case because Caracappa had never been given a warning or reprimand. . . . Thus, we have a situation where the repeated breach of the rule, if it existed, created a practice, which the workers may have been justified in believing was proper because of the failure of the employer to enforce the rule.[31]

Nevertheless, safety rule violations may be punished and punished severely, if the employer sets the example and adheres to it. The case cited below illustrates this, as well as the arbitrator's handling of a conflict of testimony. It concerned a discharge for violation of a no smoking rule in a refinery. The dismissal was based on the unsupported testimony of a general foreman who turned in two men, notwithstanding their flat denial of guilt. In dismissing the grievance, the arbitrator reasoned that:

> To rule against management in a case based solely on the personal testimony of a member of the supervisory staff as against the personal testimony of the two employees could very well, in the future, jeopardize the responsibility vested in those who direct and supervise. . . .
>
> Neither Snodgrass nor Palmer were in the same department or the same division with Mr. Frazier [the general foreman], hence the latter would have no cause or reason to be provoked with working relations of the two employees in question.
>
> The discharge penalty for violation of the no smoking rule is firmly established in practice and upheld in arbitration both for the industry and refinery.[32]

---

[31] Joseph Brandschain in *Alan Wood Steel Co. and USWA* (1946), 3 LA 557.
[33] Arbitrator Frank Wallace Naggi in *Standard Oil Co. of Indiana and Central States Petroleum Union* (1952), 5 ALAA 69,180.

The evidential problem of one man's word against another's was more subtly analyzed by Harry Shulman in a similar case several years earlier. Here the penalty was a two-week disciplinary layoff for smoking, with the union contending that the employer's position could not be maintained because "proof of [the] violation is based on the testimony of only one individual, the Plant Protection man who picked him up." This conclusion was promptly rejected:

Truth does not depend upon the number or weight of witnesses. . . . When testimony is conflicting, one can only make the best judgment possible in the circumstances. It would be improper to assume that a charge by a Plant Protection man or foreman is always true and never mistaken or unfounded. It would be at least equally improper to assume, on the other hand, that the accused's denial of the charge is always true. Experience certainly does not justify the belief that an accused, either in a plant or in the courts, always confesses his guilt, if he is guilty. Experience rather tends to a contrary conclusion. . . .

In this case I cannot conscientiously interfere with the Company's finding that the aggrieved was guilty of smoking. One cannot escape the general fact that an accused has an incentive for denying the charge, in that he stands immediately to gain or lose in the case, and that normally there is no reason why a Plant Protection man should pick one employee out of hundreds and accuse him of smoking. To be sure, this is only a general impression. In particular cases the particular accused may deny the charge with complete truthfulness. And the Plant Protection man may be mistaken or in some cases even malicious. In this case, however, there has not been even a suggestion of ill-will toward the aggrieved on the part of the Plant Protection man. Apparently they did not even know each other. No circumstances whatever appear to suggest a conclusion that the Plant Protection man was mistaken. The conclusion in these circumstances that the charge was true can hardly be deemed improper.[33]

Insubordination

Defiance of authority is a major industrial crime, for which the time-honored penalty has been summary discharge, a carry-over from military organization and the associated concept of unquestioning obedience to orders. The parallel was never too perfect— except perhaps on shipboard and in a few other employments

---

[33] *Ford Motor Co. and UAW*, Opinion A-190 (1945), in Shulman and Chamberlain, *Cases*, p. 59.

where the group hazard was similarly obvious—so that in recent years problems of insubordination have been examined more carefully, with extenuating factors given greater weight.[34] Unions, particularly, have challenged management's concept of authority and have insisted that its exercise be brought under the general rules of equity and fair play.

In industrial employment, the major forms of misconduct in this precinct are subsumed under two heads: refusal to obey, and abuse or criticism of management. However, other minor sorts of non-coöperation are also often covered by regulation. The principal forms of challenge to authority are as follows:

1. Refusal to obey or willful failure to carry out orders.

2. Criticizing, abusing, attacking, or obstructing supervision in any way.

3. Interfering with or refusing to coöperate with plant protection.

4. Refusal of identification—to show badge, explain, etc.

5. Use of company bulletin boards without authorization.

6. Bribery: making gifts or loans to supervisors.

Insubordination is the form of personal misconduct most commonly carried to arbitration, with the great majority of disputes falling into the first two classes above. The first ranges all the way from willful negligence to outright rejection of orders, whereas the second class runs the gamut from argument and a disrespectful attitude to assault. There is no question where arbitrators stand on the principle involved; the employee's duty is to obey, even if he thinks the order violates his rights under the agreement, and then grieve. The principle was elaborated at length by Shulman in a leading award in 1944,[35] and has been repeated many times since.

The employee himself must also normally obey the order, even though he thinks it improper. His remedy is prescribed in the grievance procedure. He may not take it on himself to disobey. To be sure, one can conceive of improper orders which need not be obeyed. An employee is not expected to obey an order to do that which would be

---

[34] This is especially true of nonindustrial occupations such as the civil service, private nonprofit institutions, etc.

[35] *Ford Motor Co. and UAW*, Opinion A-116 (1944), 3 LA 779, in Shulman and Chamberlain, *Cases*, p. 42.

criminal or otherwise unlawful. He may refuse to obey an improper order, which involves an unusual health hazard or other serious sacrifice. But in the absence of such justifying factors, he may not refuse to obey merely because the order violates some right of his under the Contract. The remedy under the Contract for violation of right lies in the grievance procedure and only in the grievance procedure. To refuse obedience because of a claimed contract violation would be to substitute individual action for collective bargaining and to replace the grievance procedure with extra-contractual methods. . . .

Some men apparently think that when a violation of contract seems clear, the employee may refuse to obey and thus resort to self-help rather than the grievance procedure. That is an erroneous point of view. In the first place, what appears to one party to be a clear violation may not seem so at all to the other party. Neither party can be the final judge as to whether the Contract has been violated. The determination of that issue rests in collective negotiation through the grievance procedure. . . . That procedure is prescribed for all grievances, not merely for doubtful ones. *Nothing in the Contract even suggests the idea that only doubtful violations need be processed through the grievance procedure* and that clear violations can be resisted through individual self-help. *The only difference between a "clear" violation and a "doubtful" one is that* the former makes a clear grievance and the latter a doubtful one. But *both must be handled in the regular prescribed manner.* . . .

But an industrial plant is not a debating society. Its object is production. When a controversy arises, production cannot wait for exhaustion of the grievance procedure. While that procedure is being pursued, production must go on. And some one must have the authority to direct the manner in which it is to go on until the controversy is settled. That authority is vested in Supervision. It must be vested there because the responsibility for production is also vested there; and responsibility must be accompanied by authority. It is fairly vested there because the grievance procedure is capable of adequately recompensing employees for abuse of authority by Supervision.[36]

In principle, therefore, management finds the arbitrators lined up solidly in support of its position. However, the principle and its application are two different things. Shulman himself gave the rule about its stiffest jolt in 1946, when he reinstated a group of glaziers who had been discharged for refusal of an assignment to painting when no glazing work was available.[37]

[36] See Arbitrator Jacob B. Courshon in *Torrington Co. and UAW* (1945), 1 LA 35, and many others to the same effect. (Italics mine.)

[37] *Ford Motor Co. and UAW*, Opinion A-223 (1946), 3 LA 782, in Shulman and Chamberlain, *Cases*, p. 309.

Painting and glazing are two distinct trades in skilled Maintenance or Construction work. Each classification constitutes a separate seniority group.

In this case there is no dispute as to whether the painting work to which the aggrieved were assigned could properly be considered as work within their classification. Admittedly the painting work was not part of the glazier's classification and was in no way related to it. Nor was there any emergency or unusual reason for the assignment. It is a bald case in which a skilled tradesman was assigned to work wholly different from and unrelated to his classification because of a shortage of work in his own classification or a desire to get the other work done. . . .

In these circumstances, I must hold that the aggrieved were improperly discharged and are entitled to compensation for the time lost.

Few people familiar with industrial employment would argue with the decision, but it and others like it have punched the principle of unquestioning obedience full of holes.[38] As might be expected, many such disputes arise out of conflict between supervision and union representatives in the plant. A shop steward, for instance, has certain responsibilities toward the employees in his jurisdiction covered by the agreement. How far do these responsibilities carry? May he countermand an order of a foreman when it is clearly in violation of the agreement? Certainly not, would be the probable answer. But see the decision of Arbitrator Sol I. Flink in *American Transformer Co. and UE* (1945):

Robert Blakeley was chief shop steward. On September 5, 1945, Plant Superintendent Smith notified the employees who had been working on a particular job that there was no more work for them in this department. For that reason they were not to report for work on the following day. . . . The notice was given by Smith to the

---

[38] Shulman's attempt to distinguish this case from that covered in Opinion A-116 (above, pp. 121–122) is one of the rare instances where his argument has a specious ring. Instead of meeting the issue head-on, he defended his decision as follows:

"Nothing in Opinion A-116 justifies the disciplinary action in this case. That opinion dealt primarily with production employees. It may be applied to the skilled classifications in situations *where there is reasonable dispute as to whether* the work assigned does or does not fall within the employee's classification. The duty of obedience to orders may well be extended to such instances of reasonable dispute. But it cannot be extended to assignments of work in admittedly different skilled trades constituting different seniority groups. . . . The skilled tradesman for whom there is no work in his trade is entitled to refuse a transfer to another trade in a different seniority group in which he has no seniority rights and take a layoff." (Italics mine.)

employees shortly after 4 P.M., Wednesday, September 5th. . . . When Blakeley appeared on the floor . . . he thereupon told the plant superintendent that, under Article 3 of the agreement, the company was required to give the union 24 hours' notice before any layoff could be effected and that, in the absence of such notice, the employees were entitled to compensation for half a day's work on the day following. . . .

He thereupon advised the girls to report to work the following day —"ordered" them, according to the foreman and superintendent— which they did. The company then brought charges of insubordination against Blakeley for issuing orders contrary to those of the plant superintendent and discharged him.

In the opinion of the arbitrator, Blakeley acted in accord with his responsibility as chief shop steward. . . . No allegation has been made that Blakeley used improper language. . . . It is impossible to determine at this time the exact phrase which B used in telling the workers to report for work. . . . But, even if he had done it in the form of "ordering" them to report, such choice of words . . . could not and should not be regarded as "insubordination."

For these reasons, the arbitrator finds that Blakeley was discharged without due reason, and he orders the company to reinstate Blakely with full back pay since the date of dismissal.[39]

What has probably not been sufficiently realized is that the introduction of a labor agreement produces a revolutionary change in the relationship of superior and subordinate. The first thing to go is the implicit assumption of the authoritarian tradition that "management can do no wrong." Under a union contract, it is perfectly clear that management can err, and in untold thousands of grievance proceedings management has conceded its error or been forced to reverse itself by an arbitrator's ruling. Since grievances do not materialize from thin air, but emanate from specific complaints initiated by the rank and file, a questioning attitude on the part of workers is not only tolerated, it is encouraged. It is also indisputable that a grievance or two concerning supervisory indiscretions, which have been prosecuted to a successful conclusion, do nothing at all to enhance management's claim to undisputed authority in the premises. Hence, what a few years ago might have been regarded as an intolerable impertinence coming from an employee is today far less likely to be treated as such.

---

[39] 1 LA 456.

In the second major category of insubordinate acts, experience is similar to that related previously. There is little doubt that in the great majority of cases the principle holds that "the use of abusive and threatening language toward the employer and the indulgence in excessive displays of temperament are recognized as adequate grounds for discharge." [40] However, this doctrine, like that regarding disobedience, is also something less than airtight. For example, a union steward charged with tardiness engaged in argument with his foreman, grabbed him by the arm, and threatened to "punch him in the nose." It was the second incident of its kind in four months, and there was no disagreement about the facts. The employee was known to be cocky, quick-tempered, free of speech, and generally belligerent. He was discharged. Said the arbitrator:

> However, in the final analysis, things done by Employee Kurtz and all words spoken by him, even though having a color of insubordination, consisted entirely of words and threats but no actual act of violence. . . . There is no question in the mind of the arbitrator that Employee Kurtz should be disciplined, as he was a union leader and required to set a better example. However, the penalty of complete discharge is beyond that justified under the circumstances. . . . The proper penalty . . . was suspension for a period of 30 days with loss of pay and seniority for that . . . period but without loss of . . . vacation earned. . . .[41]

In addition to the outright compromise of principle in the cases mentioned previously, there are also all the extenuating factors applicable to any form of misconduct. Authority is exercised by people. Insubordination is always man against man. It involves tempers, personalities, problems of communication, and differing points of view. Did the employee understand the order? Did he realize beyond question that he was violating it? Was he a long-service employee with an otherwise clean record? Was he ill or under strain at the time? Did he try to make amends? Was his attitude as a witness frank, straightforward, contrite? Did supervision conduct itself properly, with firmness, courtesy, and con-

---

[40] *Discharge for Cause,* by Myron Gollup, New York State Department of Labor, Division of Research and Statistics (New York: 1948), p. 58.
[41] Arbitrator Jacob B. Courshon in *Foote Bros. Gear and Machinery Corp. and UE, CIO* (1945), 1 LA 561.

cern for the employee's jeopardy? If the employee was a union official, was due allowance made for his responsibility as a representative of the employees? What was the background of relationship between the parties? Etc., etc.

Probably the key factor and the most difficult thing for an outsider to assess is the customary relationship of the parties, the "atmosphere of the shop." Whatever this may be, normally— sober and formal, relaxed and witty, profane and personal—it can be violated in ways that are hardly recognizable by nonmembers of the society and that are almost impossible of proof. To quote an arbitrator with long experience in disciplinary disputes: "Shop practice sometimes takes all the sting out of what are generally considered 'fighting words,' whereas a workman can say 'sir' to a foreman in a contemptuous and insulting manner." [42] It is a part of the art of supervision to maintain authority without being at the same time "stiff-necked," and a "heel," or a martinet. It is a part of the art of working under supervision to demonstrate respect for authority without undue subservience or loss of individuality. Neither is easy during periods of stress, which occur often enough in industrial employment. The general conclusions of arbitrators seem to be to regard discharge as a severe form of punishment for insubordination, but to let lesser penalties stand in a majority of the cases.

Jurisdiction.—Since altercations between employees and supervisors may take place after hours and off company property, the question of the limits of company jurisdiction arises. [43] The views of arbitrators on this matter are by no means uniform, but the following general rule stated in 1944 has apparently been widely accepted. An employee was discharged for waylaying a foreman outside the plant gate at the close of shift and "beating him up" because of an incident that occurred in the shop. The employee grieved on grounds of lack of company jurisdiction.

We can start with the basic premise that the Company is not entitled to use its disciplinary power for the purpose of regulating the lives and conduct of its employees outside of their employment relation. The Company does not claim any such right. . . .

---

[42] Benjamin Aaron, privately to the author.
[43] See below, this chapter, for additional comment on the problem of jurisdiction.

But the jurisdictional line which separates the cases with which the employer may be concerned from those with which he may not, is not always the physical line which bounds his property on which his plant is located. . . . No one would suggest that an employee who maliciously destroys a Company automobile while on a public highway, would not come within the range of [the rule prohibiting malicious destruction of Company property].

The point is that the jurisdictional line which limits the Company's power of discipline is a functional, not a physical line. It has power to discipline for misconduct directly related to the employment. It has no power to discipline for misconduct not related to employment. . . .

I must hold, therefore, that if a worker attacks a member of supervision or if a member of supervision attacks a worker outside the plant after working hours because of work incidents in the plant, he does so only at the risk of being disciplined by the Company for the attack. . . .[44]

Conclusions.—The main consideration in cases of challenge to managerial authority is and must be the practical one of getting things done. Nonetheless, getting things done under a labor agreement is markedly different from proceeding under unilateral control where management's word is law and no appeal may be taken. The decisions of arbitrators are clear on this point, and the precedents they have set have undoubtedly conditioned the exercise of authority throughout a wide area of industrial employment.

The statistical evidence, drawn from reported arbitrations, supports the conclusion that managerial treatment of insubordination tends to exceed the bounds of propriety. The standard remedy is discharge, but the arbitrators either reversed or modified almost two-thirds of the company rulings, which meant, at a minimum, reinstatement of the employee (see tables 10 and 11). Where the penalty was less severe, a sizable majority of the decisions were in favor of management.

What all this means is not that the plant has become "a debating society." It is still the employee's duty to obey. However, the latitude accorded management in its demand for prompt and unquestioning obedience is considerably narrowed from the practical infinity of noncontractual times, and even from the accepted

---

[44] Arbitrator Harry Shulman in *Ford Motor Co. and UAW*, Opinion A-132 (1944), in Shulman and Chamberlain, *Cases*, p. 415.

TABLE 10

PENALTIES ASSIGNED IN INSUBORDINATION CASES

Penalties	Cases	
	Number	Per cent
Discharge	122	74
Suspension........................	36	22
Reprimand........................	4	3
Transfer........................	2	1
Total........................	164[a]	

SOURCE: *Labor Arbitration Reports*, Volumes 1-10, Bureau of National Affairs.
[a] Total disagrees with the number of awards because of inclusion of more than one grievance in a single decision.

TABLE 11

ARBITRATORS' DECISIONS IN INSUBORDINATION CASES

Decisions	Cases	
	Number	Per cent
ALL TYPES		
Upheld........................	70	43
Modified........................	51	31
Reversed........................	43	26
Total........................	164	
DISCHARGE CASES		
Upheld........................	44	36
Modified........................	47	39
Reversed........................	31	25
Total........................	122	
SUSPENSION CASES		
Upheld........................	21	58
Modified........................	4	11
Reversed........................	11	31
Total........................	36	

SOURCE: *Labor Arbitration Reports*, Volumes 1-10, Bureau of National Affairs.

doctrine of "illegal or hazardous" tasks which are admittedly exceptions to the general rule. Management, as well as the work force, operates under "a higher law," consisting of limits set by the agreement, standardized practice in industry, and the general rules of fair play. Where any of these are openly violated by supervision, an employee protected by rights of tenure and accumulated seniority may interpose an objection with a minimum of peril.

The proper attitude of supervision is to regard such challenges, particularly if made without rancor, as useful warnings of the possibility of error and as opportunities for review and reconsideration. If management is in the wrong, withdrawal at an early stage is more graceful and considerably less expensive than reversal at the end of grievance proceedings and arbitration. If such reëxamination confirms the supervisor of the correctness of his action, he may insist upon compliance with more assurance than otherwise.

There is no blinking the fact that this is markedly different from the exercise of managerial authority in the absence of an agreement. However, the loss in efficiency, if any, may well be counterbalanced to a considerable extent by a better feeling, a higher morale, and eventually increased coöperation toward common goals.

Dishonesty or Disloyalty

In the environment of employment, dishonesty and disloyalty take a variety of forms which have been spelled out in detail in company rules. The most important categories are the following:

1. Theft or unauthorized removal of company property from premises.

2. Use or possession of unassigned plant material or equipment.

3. Use or possession of another employee's tools or property without consent.

4. Falsifying production records or concealing defective work.

5. Falsification of personnel or other company records.

6. Punching the time card of another employee or permitting another to punch one's own card.

7. Lending or borrowing a badge without authorization.

8. Disclosure of confidential information to competitors or other unauthorized persons.

9. False, vicious, or malicious statements about the company or its products.

Neither dishonesty nor disloyalty calls for much explanation as a basis for disciplinary action. Both are sufficiently undesirable character attributes to support very severe penalties. However, the issue is seldom unclouded. There are degrees of both dishonesty and disloyalty, as well as proof of same, and a multiplicity of factors may enter into the judgment. Moreover, in an atmosphere of protected employee rights, the very gravity of the charge is itself a form of safeguard. As pointed out in an early case,[45] the consequences are so serious to the employee both in terms of material loss (seniority rights, etc.) and of damage to his reputation, that the burden of proof is on the company to present clear and convincing evidence of guilt sufficient to justify the action taken.

This particular dispute was over a discharge for falsification of an employment application, and the dismissal came after thirteen months of satisfactory service. The arbitrator observed that the application blank was a printed form, prepared by the company and designed to afford the employer the maximum protection and advantage, with some of the applicant's major obligations and responsibilities for full disclosure stated in legal terms in a section of very fine print. The customary rule of both law and equity, it was pointed out, is to construe such a document most strongly against the employer.

And finally, there was the matter of intent. If the applicant's suppression of information or misstatements were clearly intended to influence the company to hire him, then they were material. If not, they could not be termed "consequential omissions" and held against him. Finding the evidence on this score dubious, the arbitrator reversed the company and reinstated the employee, at the same time quoting with approval Shulman's rule of a statute of limitations.[46]

---

[45] Arbitrator Benjamin Aaron in *Aviation Maintenance Corp. and IAM* (1947), 8 LA 261.
[46] See above, chap. iii.

Dishonesty and disloyalty are general attributes; what they mean in specific cases depends on the industry, the company, and the situation. In the meat-packing industry, theft is a serious matter and is usually dealt with by discharge. Thus, an employee with a ten-year service record was dismissed for appropriating 1½ pounds of meat, which he attempted to explain on grounds of forgetting to bring his lunch to work. The arbitrator was impressed:

I am of the opinion that disciplinary action was warranted. But I am also of the view that since the Company does not dispute the ten and a half years of satisfactory service by Licciardi, some consideration might well have been given this factor. The testimony of Licciardi and of his son that he forgot his lunch, the testimony that employees do eat processed meats when they are hungry . . . all appear to me to warrant further consideration by the Company.

Award: In view of the above facts and conclusions, I find that . . . the proper disposition of this case will be to reëmploy him with the understanding that the record is not cleared thereby, and that no precedent is being established for the future.[47]

Where the facts are in dispute, the burden is on the employer to make a convincing case against the employee. In another packing house case, an employee was accused by a plant policeman of taking a bite of sausage. He was taken to the office, reported, suspended for a week, told that nothing he could say would change the decision, and escorted to the dressing room by a second officer. In testimony at the hearing, the employee said that both policemen had liquor on their breaths, and he therefore concluded that a protest would be unavailing at the time. Neither policeman appeared at the hearing. The arbitrator's opinion was brief and pointed.

The remarkable feature of this case is Carr's testimony to the effect that the two police officers who preferred charges against him were under the influence of liquor; that under those circumstances he considered it futile to argue with them or press his claim to innocence; and that he was suspended without a hearing and without any opportunity to state his defense. This testimony stands unrebutted since the two policemen did not present themselves at the hearing. . . . The Company's failure to present as witnesses the only two persons who

[47] Arbitrator A. Howard Myers in *Boston Sausage and Provision Co. and UPWA* (1947), 8 LA 483.

witnessed the incident shuts out the possibility of giving any consideration to the merit of the Company's position.[48]

A major difficulty in dishonesty and disloyalty cases is the
evidence. It is often circumstantial and just as often conflicting.
The opinions of the arbitrators are in agreement that it must be
at least preponderant. Although these charges are near the top of
the list of industrial crimes in seriousness, in the published
awards, at least, a lower proportion of penalties is upheld than
in any other major area of misconduct (see tables 12 and 13).

Immoral, Illegal, Subversive Activity

This is a general catchall of what are sometimes termed "grave
offenses," objectionable in themselves or violative of civil or
criminal statutes. Although the possibility of loss or hazard to the
company is implicit in some cases, it is absent in others (for
example, gambling) except by indirection. The essential element
throughout is some kind of violation of the general moral standards of the community. The arguable basis for discharge, the
usual penalty, might be the reflection cast on the organization
by the deeds of the members, but the necessity for such a defense
varies with the situation. Presumably, it is within the province
of a firm to insist that its employees be of good moral character,
at least while on the job, and most of the offenses in this class
admittedly would not fit such a description.

Subversive activity.—One test of good moral character that is
not within the province of the private employer as a general
matter is disloyalty. In recent years, with national security an
important issue and with defense contracts and subcontracts widespread throughout the industrial community, discharge on
grounds of subversive activity has become a frequent source
of grievance. Arbitrators are in very close agreement as to the
basic rule: a private employer may not fire an employee for
disloyalty, Communist Party membership, or "taking the Fifth
Amendment," unless it can be shown that the worker's activities
violate a plant rule or are demonstrably harmful to the firm's

---

[48] Arbitrator Harold M. Gilden in *Armour and Co. and UPWA* (1948), 9 LA
904.

TABLE 12

PENALTIES ASSIGNED IN DISHONESTY AND DISLOYALTY CASES

Penalties	Cases	
	Number	Per cent
Discharge	28	82
Suspension	4	12
Fine	1	3
Demotion	1	3
Total	34[a]	

SOURCE: *Labor Arbitration Reports*, Volumes 1–10, Bureau of National Affairs.
[a] Total disagrees with the number of awards because of inclusion of more than one grievance in a single decision.

TABLE 13

ARBITRATORS' DECISIONS IN DISHONESTY AND DISLOYALTY CASES

Decisions	Cases	
	Number	Per cent
ALL TYPES		
Upheld	10	30
Modified	12	35
Reversed	12	35
Total	34	
DISCHARGE CASES		
Upheld	8	29
Modified	12	42
Reversed	8	29
Total	28	

SOURCE: *Labor Arbitration Reports*, Volumes 1–10, Bureau of National Affairs.

business.[49] The rule is grounded on the responsibility of the civil authorities for the relationship between the individual and the

[49] See *Consolidated Western Steel Corp. and United Steelworkers* (1949), 13 LA 721, Arbitrator Spencer Pollard; *Foote Bros. Gear and Machinery Corp.* (1949), 13 LA 848, Arbitrator John Day Larkin; *Bell Aircraft Corp. and UAW* (1951), 16 LA 234, Arbitrator Joseph Shister.

government, the legality of Communist Party membership, and the constitutional rights of citizens not to incriminate themselves.

Exceptions to the rule are permissible if the activity is clearly proved and jeopardy to the employer's business is established. For example, open and obvious Communist Party membership combined with taking refuge behind the Fifth Amendment in response to questions of a public investigating committee may properly be held to be incompatible with editorship of a newspaper.[50] Likewise, a directive from a government agency with which the employer has a defense contract to remove an employee from access to classified material may be sufficient grounds for discharge.

The jurisdictional issue.—A major problem in cases involving immoral, illegal, or subversive activity is to draw the boundaries of the company's jurisdiction. Some of the named offenses are clearly outside the firm's area of control: criminal activity during off hours, membership in a subversive organization, morals charges, and the like. Excessive indulgence in drink, drugs, gambling, might easily bring an employee into disrepute in the community, and perhaps furnish grounds for disciplinary action. Where there is a direct carry-over to the job—Monday morning hang-overs, for example—corrective action is on firm ground. Short of this, the issue is delicate and circumstances will control.

A very complete discussion of the issue of jurisdiction is found in the award of Arthur M. Ross, Chairman of Arbitration Board, in Union Oil Company of California and Oil Workers International Union, Local No. 326, to wit:

PRIVATE CONDUCT AS CAUSE FOR DISCHARGE

To what extent does an employer have a proper concern with the conduct of his employees outside of working hours and away from company property? This question has frequently arisen in arbitration cases, and a very consistent line of thinking is found in the published awards. This is significant not in creating precedents—because the force of precedent is very weak in the field of arbitration—but in showing that many thoughtful and experienced arbitrators have reached similar conclusions on the point.

---

[50] Chairman Paul A. Dodd in *Los Angeles Daily News and Los Angeles Newspaper Guild* (1952), 19 LA 39.

As a general proposition it may be stated that an employee's private conduct is of proper concern to his employer only when some legitimate interest of the employer is injured or jeopardized. Otherwise a heavy line must be drawn between the employee's occupational and non-occupational activities. His time belongs to the employer while he is on the job; but the employer does not purchase his leisure time and does not have jurisdiction or control over the use of it. Indeed, an employer could hardly assume authority over the employee's life away from the job without assuming equal responsibility for his welfare and happiness. Once a worker leaves his place of employment, the proper agency of social control is civil authority. . . .

[However] . . . , an employer does have a rightful concern with an employee's outside activities when his own legitimate interests are affected. Specifically,

1. The Company's reputation may be damaged by the notoriety. . . .

2. The employee's outside activities may involve the employer in excessive bookkeeping, legal expenses, etc. . . . [Garnishments, etc.]

3. Misconduct off the job may destroy an employee's efficiency on the job. . . .

4. Misconduct off the job may constitute sufficient evidence that an employee is not qualified for his specific assignment. . . . [A showing of irresponsibility, for example.]

5. The employee's presence in the plant may disrupt production and demoralize the working force. . . .

6. The employee's outside activities may damage the employer's business interests. . . . [Operating a business in competition with employer.]

7. Misconduct off the premises may be integrally connected with the employment relationship. . . . [Assault on a supervisor.]

Many disciplinary actions in the area of "grave offenses" arise out of charges of drinking or gambling. Where it is the former, the question of proof is paramount, especially where the rule reads "intoxication." Even in cases of "drinking or possession," a full rundown of the available facts may produce different interpretations by different parties. For instance, a machinist employed by a distillery and with a ten-year record of good service was discharged for violation of a rule covering "drinking alcoholic beverages or found to be in possession of alcoholic beverages other than in the normal conduct of work."[51]

---

[51] *Joseph E. Seagram & Sons and IAM* (1946), 1 ALAA 67,386, Arbitrator L. C. Willis.

The evidence produced by the company supervisor was to the effect that Ellis was found reaching behind a glass hopper and upon being asked by the supervisor what he was doing replied that he was putting the bottle containing the whiskey behind the hopper. Ellis stated that while engaged in sweeping up glass, he noticed the bottle sitting there and picked it up and looked at it and placed it back. This was corroborated by W. D. Cecil. Miss Daniels, under cross examination, admitted that Mr. Cecil was present and heard her conversation with Mr. Ellis. . . .

It has long been established in the law that one accused of a misdeed must have performed the act with a criminal intent and that before he can be convicted thereof the evidence must show beyond a reasonable doubt that he is guilty. It is the opinion of the undersigned that the evidence in this case materially fails to show any intention to violate the rule involved, and further that the evidence of the accused raises such a doubt in the mind of the arbitrator that he could not be found guilty.

In both drinking and gambling cases, not only must the proof be conclusive, but also the rule should fit the charge without stretching. An example of strict construction of a rule against the employer is the following:

This case involves two appeals from the Highland Park plant. . . . In the first, the aggrieved employees were playing cards—not gambling—during their lunch period. They were taken to the Labor Relations office, reprimanded and assessed one half hour for the time spent in that office. In the second case, the aggrieved employees, having reported for work early, were playing cards—not gambling—in the lunch room before their shift began. . . .

Now Exhibit A [the Company Rules] prohibits "gambling on Company property" whether on Company time or on the employees' own time. Card playing is, of course, a very common means of gambling. But cards are also commonly played without any gambling. While gambling on the employer's property is fairly generally prohibited in industry, card playing without gambling is not so proscribed. The Exhibit's rule against gambling seems to me to cover the entire field of interdicted playing. There would be little point in specifically prohibiting this form of playing if all forms of it were also prohibited. I must conclude, then, that in prohibiting gambling, the Contract impliedly permits card playing without gambling. . . . Therefore, I hold that the penalty for card playing cannot be sustained.[52]

---

[52] Umpire Harry Shulman in *Ford Motor Co. and UAW*, Opinion A-133 (1944), in Shulman and Chamberlain, *Cases*, p. 398. This is an example of application of the rule of "inclusio unius est exclusio alterius," or "to include one thing is to exclude the other."

Extenuating circumstances also play a prominent part in decisions of this type. An example is the discharge of two Greyhound bus operators for drinking while in uniform, with the additional charge of "conduct unbecoming a gentleman" (fighting) lodged against one of them. Both men were at the end of runs, away from home and on two-hour call, although the dispatcher had indicated that neither would probably be sent out for at least twelve or fourteen hours. They first drank coffee and then had three or four beers together, following which one of them had an altercation with a local resident that called for settlement by combat. The company rules against fighting or the drinking of "any alcoholic liquor or beverage . . . while in uniform at any time" were explicit. Nonetheless, the arbitrator reduced the penalty to reinstatement without back pay to the bottom of the extra board. He supported the decision with an unusually complete list of mitigating factors:

What are the extenuating circumstances in this case? In the first place, these men both have good records, are admitted by the company to be good employees, and one has had two safety awards.

To the arbitrator, these are considerations which weigh heavily in their favor and should be given substantive weight in considering the degree and nature of discipline to be administered.

Secondly: The Company does not contend that the men were intoxicated or under influence of liquor.

Thirdly: By the time either or both of the men would have been called to take out their respective runs, there is no question but that they were in fit condition in every way to operate the buses. This is not denied by the employer.

Fourthly: This was their first offense, and no similar penalty had been meted out in this . . . Region of the Company in recent years . . .

Fifthly: There is some extenuation in the fact that these men are away from home without facilities to change clothing for a good many hours, on their own time for which they are not being paid by the Company, and that it is difficult for the flesh to withstand the temptation of socializing, and taking just one glass of beer, during the long hours with nothing to do.

Lastly, and perhaps most important, the arbitrator has been very much impressed with these two men. . . . Both of them came to the arbitration hearing and pleaded for their jobs back. They ate humble pie. It took courage for them to do this, but at the same time they did it with dignity and without groveling.[53]

The statistics of reported arbitration awards relative to "grave offenses" show discharge to be the standard penalty, with about the usual proportion of decisions (two out of five) upholding the employer. (See tables 14 and 15.)

Rules and Their Administration: Summary

Nowadays, very few firms of any size attempt to operate without at least a few formal rules of conduct, and the list of both companies and of rules seems likely to lengthen rather than diminish. If employees are expected while on the job either to do or not do something which is permissible off the job or in other employments, the decision needs to be announced publicly. Otherwise, management will have to argue the reason for the rule each time it is applied. Many rules are of this sort: badges, phone use, smoking, and so on. Then, if a limited list is published, does this imply exemption of other forms of conduct which may be considered inimical to the organization? The argument leads naturally to as inclusive a list as possible, with an open-end clause to catch omissions. It has been strengthened by the demands of grievance bargaining and arbitration for definiteness and consistency.

The primary test of rule administration, as of any other managerial decision affecting employees, is fair play, but it must be admitted that enforcement of a schedule raises technical problems of due process. Not only do questions of definition arise (fighting vs. assault, card-playing vs. gambling, etc.), but also the methods of adoption, publication, and amendment of the rules may be attacked. The regulations themselves must fit into a framework of negotiation and agreement, and their enforcement will be checked against the pattern of past practice in the firm—inconsistency, condonation, allowance for mitigating circumstance. The variables are numerous and any one of them may be decisive in a given situation.

---

[53] Arbitrator Joseph Brandschain in *Pennsylvania Greyhound Lines and Amal. Assn. of Street, Elec. Ry., and Mtr. Coach Employees* (1946), 3 LA 880, in Shulman and Chamberlain, *Cases*, p. 536.

TABLE 14

PENALTIES ASSIGNED IN IMMORAL, ETC. CASES

Penalties	Cases	
	Number	Per cent
Discharge........................	22	91
Suspension.......................	2	9
Total........................	24[a]	

SOURCE: *Labor Arbitration Reports*, Volumes 1–10, Bureau of National Affairs.
[a] Total disagrees with the number of awards, because of inclusion of more than one grievance in a single decision.

TABLE 15

ARBITRATORS' DECISIONS IN IMMORAL, ETC. CASES

Decisions	Cases	
	Number	Per cent
ALL TYPES		
Upheld...........................	10	42
Modified..........................	9	37
Reversed..........................	5	21
Total........................	24	
DISCHARGE CASES		
Upheld...........................	9	41
Modified..........................	9	41
Reversed..........................	4	18
Total........................	22	

SOURCE: *Labor Arbitration Reports*, Volumes 1–10, Bureau of National Affairs.

In the chain of events that adds up to enforcement of the rules, nothing is more crucial for the rights of the employee than the procedure followed by the employer. If due process means anything, it means a public procedure. Publicity in turn means that all cards must be on the table: private, subjective motivations are likely to be thrown out or charged against the concealer, and the accused must be given an opportunity to explain or refute anything that puts him in jeopardy. This privilege must be accorded him as demerits accumulate and not be disclosed for the first time when a major disciplinary action occurs. As pointed out by Benjamin Aaron:

> Notice of charges, delivered orally in rapid-fire order to the employee at the time he is advised of the Company's decision to discipline him, is really no notice at all. The purpose of notice is to allow time for preparation, discussions with advisors, and careful consideration of the substance and form of the reply.[54]

A major hazard for employers in misconduct cases has been the nature and sufficiency of the evidence. Proper attention to the evidence means more than just being sure to make a good case. It implies taking a judicial attitude. Put bluntly, it suggests that management should, in every case, before any penalty is imposed, at least consider the possibility that it is in the wrong. Someone should look at the evidence as impartially as possible, setting aside the preconception that "management should uphold supervision," and ask himself the question: "Does this really add up?" To "add up," the evidence should be relevant, credible, objective, and preponderant. It should be: (1) directly related to the offense as charged and not a shotgun accumulation of various misdeeds (perhaps hurriedly accumulated to support the case), some of which are to the point and others far afield; (2) worthy of belief and not absurd, illogical, or contradictory; (3) factually provable, and not composed mainly of unsupported opinions, hearsay, and gossip; and (4) substantial enough, in weight of testimony, records, and/or incidents to justify both the charge and the penalty. If it fails in any of these respects, management would be wise to discover the fact itself, with a consequent saving in costs and prestige.

Finally, there is much to be said for letting the union share the responsibility throughout. Due process implies neither more nor less than seeing that employees are treated fairly for alleged rule violations. The union has an interest in good conduct as well as the employer. It is signatory to the agreement and has repre-

---

[54] *San Diego Electric Railway and Amal. Assn. of Street, Elec. Ry. and Mtr. Coach Employees* (1948), 10 LA 119.

sentatives on the ground, charged with responsibility for investigating and processing employee appeals. It has channels of communication not available to the employer, just as the employer has information not available to the union. If the objective is equity, the two parties together can do a better job than working separately and in opposition. That is the theory underlying the grievance procedure, and it is a theory that works. There is no obvious reason why the same theory should not apply to prior notification and consultation, as well as to joint rule formulation and interpretation.

Chapter VI	*Grounds for*
	Discipline:
	Violation of
	the Agreement

Violation of the agreement is the most serious kind of employee misdemeanor. Its most important form is a work stoppage of some sort, but it also includes improper acts of union representatives. The gravity of the offense stems from two factors: it jeopardizes relations between the contracting parties, that is, it may terminate the agreement; and its essential element is group insubordination, which is a genuine threat to managerial authority.

The strike is organized labor's primary weapon. As a practical matter, it is recognized that work stoppages seldom occur spontaneously, no matter how widespread or serious the dissatisfaction with management. They are instigated, that is, planned, "talked up," argued over, voted on, and led. Instigation or leadership, of course, is often very difficult to prove. One of management's thorniest problems is to separate leaders from followers and assess penalties appropriate to the degree of participation. The issue is complicated by: (1) the strong feelings aroused on both sides; (2) the ragged lines of demarcation between instigation, active support, passive agreement, and "negative" involvement (meaning the employee who opposes the action but "goes along" with his fellow workers when the chips are down); (3) official union action at various levels of authority—plant, local, international; (4) the handicaps to investigation and accumulation of evidence, much of which concerns internal union affairs;

and (5) the special duties, responsibilities, and liabilities of the parties as spelled out in the agreement and in regulatory legislation, notably the Labor Management Relations Act.

Improper acts by union representatives mean a wrongful exercise of the authority granted them as officials in the plant. What is, "wrongful," however, may be a very delicate question. It is the duty of the shop steward to act as spokesman for and adviser to the employees in his district, to "police" the contract and report violations to higher union officials, to investigate grievances, and to put the dispute machinery in motion when necessary. If he does this in the proper manner, he is immune to discipline, no matter how offensive the results may be to the employer. A "proper manner," in turn, may be considerably at variance from the correct attitude of a regular employee, which the steward is when not engaged in union duties.

While conferring with management about grievances formally and officially, the union conferee's position is that of an equal and independent party rather than that of a subordinate. The adjustment of disputes is not a part of employment for which the steward is subject to management's discipline. The very nature of the function demands the exercise of independent initiative and judgment. Therefore, in a grievance conference, for example, the display of conduct of the shop steward toward the employer, which would amount to insubordination if exhibited during the regular course of employment, has been held not to be insubordination.[1]

It is common for labor agreements to specify a number of privileges and immunities for union representatives that are not accorded other employees in the bargaining unit. They are freed from their regular jobs when the need arises to represent employees charged with delinquency or to investigate grievances, and the time thus spent is often paid for by the employer. They are customarily granted top seniority in their districts, protected from transfer out of the jurisdiction, permitted long leaves of absence, and have more freedom of movement about the plant while on union business than is granted to regular employees. The possibilities of abuse are numerous, including excessive time spent away from production, immoderate attitudes of independence

---

[1] *Discharge for Cause*, by Myron Gollub, New York State Department of Labor, Division of Research and Statistics (New York: 1948), p. 79.

of or criticism of management, interference with supervision, and recruiting or soliciting for the union during working hours.

Striking or Instigating a Strike or Slowdown

There are a large number and a very wide variety of provisions in labor agreements limiting the right to strike or lock out, and providing for specific enforcement of the contract. For example:

> In the event of a violation of the agreement, either party may have the express right to terminate the agreement, or to void the "no strike, no lock-out" pledge. The union may have the right to withdraw the union label or shop card; the employer, to cease processing grievances.[2]

These are supplemented by further restrictions in labor legislation, notably the Labor Management Relations Act.[3]

The most common arrangement in union contracts is probably the "no-strike, no-lockout" clause combined with a full grievance procedure ending in arbitration.[4] Sometimes the *quid pro quo* is made very explicit, as in the following:

> During the term of this agreement there shall be no strikes, slow-downs, picketings, stoppages of work or boycotts by the Union or its members, unless the Employer shall fail to abide by the decision of a duly constituted Board of Arbitration. There shall be no lockout by the Employer unless members of the Union shall fail to abide by the decision of a duly constituted Board of Arbitration.[5]

In other cases, the liability of the union may be limited by an express assumption of its responsibility for helping to end a walk-

---

[2] Commerce Clearing House, *Clauses*, p. 678.

[3] "Generally speaking, the Act prohibits jurisdictional strikes, secondary boycotts, strikes by the employees of an employer to compel another employer to recognize or bargain with a union as the representative of his employees unless such union has been certified as bargaining agent, and strikes to compel recognition or bargaining rights from any employer whose employees are already represented by a certified union. The Act bans strikes and lock-outs during a 60-day period prior to contact termination or modification [etc.] . . .

"The Act permits either party to bring suit in a Federal District Court for damages suffered by a strike or lock-out in violation of the contract. . . . In addition . . . there are also specific state laws and state labor relations acts in certain states which deal with the subject of strikes. . . ." *Ibid.*, pp. 667–68.

[4] "Contracts which make arbitration the final step in the grievance procedure generally prohibit for the life of the agreement or at least until all grievance machinery has been used, strikes or lockouts over arbitrable issues." Frank Elkouri, *How Arbitration Works* (Washington: Bureau of National Affairs, 1952), p. 7.

[5] Commerce Clearing House, *Clauses*, p. 676.

out and the granting to the employer of a wider range of discretion in disciplinary action:

During the term of this Agreement the Union guarantees the company on behalf of itself and each of its members that: There will be no authorized strike of any kind, boycott, picketing, work stoppage, slowdown or any other type of organized interference, coercive or otherwise, with the Company's business.

In the event any violation of the previous paragraph occurs which is unauthorized by the Union, the Company agrees that there shall be no liability on the part of the International or local union or any of the officers or agents, provided that . . . the Union first meets the following conditions:

The Union shall declare publicly that such action is unauthorized;

The Union shall promptly order its members to return to work, notwithstanding the existence of any wildcat picket line;

The Union shall not question the unqualified right of the Company to discipline or discharge employees engaging in . . . such action. It is understood that such action on the part of the company shall be final and binding upon the Union, and its members, and shall in no case be construed as a violation by the Company of this Agreement. However, an issue of fact as to whether or not any particular employee has engaged in, participated in, or encouraged any such violation, may be subject to the Grievance Procedure and/or arbitration.[6]

Whatever the language of the contract, a work stoppage during the term of the agreement is a serious matter for the employer and is usually met with prompt and stringent action. Difficulties may arise at the outset, however, in deciding whether or not a work stoppage or slowdown has taken place. For example:

About March 1, 1952, the Company began changing from cotton fabric to rayon fabric on Code 10 tires. The only change that this made in the job content was that a breaker strip was found not to be necessary, which reduced the time necessary to build a tire. Under the contract requirement that when the job content is changed the rate shall be changed commensurate with the change in job content, the Company

---

[6] *Ibid.* For a succinct but detailed summary of the many kinds of provisions governing strikes and lockouts and contract enforcement, see *ibid.*, pp. 667–673 and 677–682.

I am indebted to Professor Arthur M. Ross for the explanation that limited liability clauses such as the above were developed to meet the "agency" provisions (Sec. 301 of Title III) of the Taft-Hartley Act.

calculated that the Builders could build 160.6 tires in the same time that they had formerly built 152 tires. In other words, the reduced time permitted the building of 8.6 additional tires per shift. The rate was therefore set for the production of 160 tires per shift, the decimal being dropped, and the rate was put into effect March 14. Instead of building 160 tires per shift, the Tire Builders dropped their production far below the 155 tires which they had been building.

There were consultations with the employees and union representatives, after which production rose to its former rate of 152 but no higher. After the rate held there for a time, the company warned the employees of disciplinary action and then laid them off for three days. Upon their return, production rose to 155 tires per shift, which was followed by more talks, consultations, and warnings. With no result, the employees were laid off for thirty days, whereupon they grieved. The arbitrator observed that:

The Union made no effort to attack the correctness of the Company's computations showing that 160.6 tires could be built now in the same time that was formerly required to build 152 tires. The sole evidence of the Union consisted of statements to the effect that they could not build more than 155 tires. The contract explicitly gives to the Union the right to have its own time-study man come into the Plant to make time studies as the basis for attacks upon rates and work-loads. In spite of having this right, the Union offered no evidence to show that the rate was wrong or the work-load unreasonable.

More striking than this, but perhaps no more important, is the fact that 18 or 20 Tire Builders all built exactly the same number of tires per shift. When they were building 152 tires per shift, each of them built 152 tires per shift, and when they went up to 155 tires, each of them built 155 tires. Such uniformity is consistent only with concerted agreement. Men's abilities and speeds and efficiencies differ. If 20 Tire Builders were building according to their individual abilities, production would vary among them. When each has exactly the same production, the conclusion is inevitable that they have agreed upon that production. When men agree to limit their production below what is a fair and normal work-load, it constitutes a slowdown. The Union inquired at the Hearing how they could be accused of slowing down when they increased production from 152 to 155 tires. Whether they slowed down or not, is not a question of the specific number of tires produced, but of effort expended. They slowed down their efforts. . . . These men were given ample warning, and their continuance of contract violation after warning quite clearly justified the Company in taking the disciplinary action that it took. For these reasons the grievances will be dismissed.[7]

No two work stoppages are alike and problems of definition may be crucial when related to contract terminology. For example, is a series of concerted work interruptions for "union meetings," combined with unannounced late reporting of whole shifts, occurring at three widely separated plants, a strike? These took place during wage-reopener negotiations under an agreement that permitted the union to strike after thirty days of fruitless bargaining but barred the company from use of the lockout under any circumstances. When the company closed its plants, following a series of protests against the irregularities, the union grieved, claiming a lockout. After extensive hearings and review of testimony, the arbitrator held that neither a strike nor a lockout had occurred, that the company's closing of its plants was not a lockout to force the concessions but a defensive action to avoid economic loss and therefore permissible.[8]

Condonation, discrimination, extenuating circumstances.— Discipline for contract violation, as for any other type of misdemeanor, is subject to condonation, discrimination, and mitigating circumstances. If the company has made a practice of permitting employees to walk off the job in protest without subsequent penalty, it is in a difficult position later on when it decides to treat such action as a violation of the agreement. On July 31, 1952, five men on the "Draw gang" of the Belden Brick Company became dissatisfied with the assignment of a replacement employee to the gang. They "sat down" on the job, while two of their number went to protest to the plant superintendent, and when the two returned all of them rang out and went home. When they returned to work the following morning, they "found that their cards had been removed from the rack and that the company considered that they had quit voluntarily and refused to reinstate them."[9] They grieved, basing their complaints on the fact that

---

[7] Arbitrator Whitley P. McCoy in *Goodyear Tire and Rubber Co. and United Rubber, Cork, Linoleum, and Plastic Workers of America* (1952), 5 ALAA 69,015.

[8] Arbitrator James J. Healy in *General Cable Corp. and United Electrical, Radio, and Machine Workers of America* (1952), 5 ALAA 69,048.

[9] *Belden Brick Co. and United Brick and Clay Workers* (1952), 5 ALAA 69,203, G. Seinsheimer, Impartial Chairman.

there had been similar occurrences in the past, for which no penalty had been exacted. This was confirmed at the hearing:

Cross examination of B. B. Wentz, the general superintendent, brought out that following a similar "sit down" and walk off the job in May that he issued instructions that if it occurred again that the men's cards were to be pulled and the men treated as if they had quit their jobs. It was further admitted by supervision that the men who had quit in May were put back to work without penalty. It was also admitted that no notice was posted or verbal caution given that if the walk offs occurred again that the men would not be taken back.

Holding that both management and men were to blame, the arbitrator awarded the men back pay from the time of dismissal until they got other jobs (all were reëmployed at the time), but held that the company was not required to reinstate them.

When a misdemeanor is a joint project (as in a strike), the relationship of each penalty to the others is brought into sharp relief. If the relationship is out of line, the punishment is inconsistent. Thus, after an unauthorized work stoppage at the Fruehauf Trailer Company, two stewards were discharged for leading the walkout. After reviewing the evidence, the arbitrator commuted the penalties to disciplinary layoff, arguing that:

In this case, the president of the local union has admitted that he authorized the walkout and has accepted the responsibility for the strike, but he was not discharged. How, then, can one fairly sustain the discharge of lesser union officials who, at most, were carrying out his instructions?

G . . . had no part in the instigation, direction, or leadership of the strike. He was guilty of at least one overt act. . . . Several other employees were as culpable as he if not more so. [Two weeks suspension.] M did have a part in the leadership of the strike. Except for his actions, it is unlikely that any employees of the department, except those in his own district, would have walked out. . . . The only reason for not sustaining his discharge is that the union president was not discharged. . . . [Reinstatement with one-half back pay.][10]

The issue of discrimination, however, is restricted to matters within the employer's knowledge. In a mass action such as a strike, the latter is not required to ferret out and prove every

[10] Arbitrator Dudley E. Whiting in *Freuhauf Trailer Co. and UAW* (1946), 1 LA 506.

violation. The probability or even the certainty of equal guilt of some of the parties going unpunished will not void the action taken if it can be supported on its merits.

Undoubtedly there were other employees who played a prominent role in the . . . violation of the agreement. The fact that the Company has not presented a case against such individuals does not sustain a charge of discrimination, in the absence of a showing of discrimination *against* the aggrieved employees. The Company is not a law enforcement agency charged with the sworn duty of detecting each violator of a given statute. In the case of an unauthorized strike, without the coöperation of the Union in locating those who have the major responsibility for the violation of the Agreement, the Company in imposing discipline is limited practically to those against whom its charges can be fully supported. The mere fact that there may have been other employees who may have been equally guilty does not make the act of the Company discriminatory.[11]

The influence of extenuating circumstances is illustrated in a case involving the Atlantic Parachute Corp. of Lowell, Massachusetts, and the Amalgamated Clothing Workers of America:

Twelve workers, titled Main Seam Operators, who were dissatisfied with the piece rate set by the Company on that operation, which was newly introduced the latter part of June and was in process only a limited time . . . took it upon themselves to walk off their job on July 28, 1952, engaging in a strike in violation of the contract. . . .[12]

They were discharged, but "after being out of the plant for five working days, returned to their jobs and were permitted by the Company to work as new employees. . . ." The union interceded for the men, asking restoration of seniority on grounds that they admitted their mistake and promised never to repeat the offense. It was finally left up to the arbitrator, who, reflecting upon the promises of the men and the fact that this was the first contract violation on record, reduced the penalty to a loss of ninety days' seniority.

---

[11] Herbert Blumer, Chairman of Board of Arbitration, in *Carnegie-Illinois Steel Corp. and USWA* (1946), 5 LA 363, in Shulman and Chamberlain, *Cases*, p. 422. See also: *Chrysler Corp. and UAW* (1952), 5 ALAA 68,974, Arbitrator David A. Wolff, and *International Harvester Co. and UAW* (1952), 5 ALAA 69,058, Arbitrator Ray Forrester, for examples of commutation of discharges on account of inconsistency of penalties.

[12] Arbitrator Maxwell Copelof (1952), 5 ALAA 69,185.

Instigation and leadership.—In assessing blame for unauthorized work stoppages, a key question is leadership. Under the circumstances, it is natural for management to check closely on union representatives in whose jurisdictions the walkouts occur. If they appear to be actively involved, as joining, assisting, or heading up the movement, they are practically sure to be singled out for severe punishment. The reason for this is not only suspicion of the union and its leaders in any combined action (although such suspicion undoubtedly prevails), it is also the fact that the officers of the union are obligated to uphold the contract and are often committed by the agreement to taking positive steps to avoid a breach or end a walkout.[13] Where not positively committed by contract, they have usually been held by arbitrators to have such obligations. This principle was elaborated in an early decision by Shulman, after a group of employees had been discharged on account of a work stoppage accompanied by picketing.

The two-day stoppage and picketing were, of course, in complete disregard of the Union's Constitution. No effort was made to secure authorization from the International or otherwise to follow the constitutional requirements. Representatives of the International and officers of the Local were promptly on the scene and urged the employees to return to work; but their efforts were rebuffed. . . . Two of the aggrieved employees were Building Chairmen. Several were committeemen. Their obligation to comply with the Contract and Constitution was even greater than that of the rank and file employees. Their office imposes upon them additional duties as well as privileges. They were required to be more conversant with the Contract. Their constituents look to them for guidance and example. Their actions affect the conduct of others and the honor of the Union to a far greater extent than do those of the rank and file.

One of the committeemen explained his credo as follows: he is opposed to wildcat, unauthorized strikes and would accordingly do all he could to dissuade employees from engaging in them; but if his advice goes unheeded and the employees form a picket line, his place is in the line with them.

This is a romantic expression of a perverse and debasing view of the committeeman's obligations. A committeeman is not merely a friend

---

[13] Such clauses or others like them are found in many agreements. An example is the *Agreement between North American Aviation, Inc., and the United Automobile Workers, Effective March 19, 1956*, p. 44.

of the employees, tied to them by bonds of sympathy and loyalty. He is also a Union member and a Union official. He has taken his "obligation" to the Union; and, through the Union, he has pledged his honor and assumed the legal duty to observe the Contract with the Company. It is not a breach of his loyalty to his men to insist that they perform their duties and "bring (no) reproach upon" their Union, or to refuse to lead or join them in contrary conduct. Indeed, true loyalty to his men, as well as to his Union and to the Contract, requires him to do just that; and to do it at the very time when his men are disinclined to heed his advice. . . . If he fails to do this, he is at least not to join and give them leadership.[14]

This is an important principle and clearly a correct one. If union representatives meet Shulman's test, there will be fewer work stoppages in violation of contract. When they do occur, the rule will help to focus responsibility and narrow the range of evidence required to establish guilt. However, it will not work automatically; the difficult question of evidence is still prominent and there is plenty of room within the rule for contrary findings of fact. This is well illustrated in a case involving discharge for a series of work stoppages in one division of a steel mill.

The charges of the Company against Mr. Bral rest primarily on the ground of his position of leadership in the Union. . . . Mr. Bral was the Grievance Committeeman for the Cold Roll Division. It was only the workers of this Division who were involved in the work stoppages. In its major character, the case of the Company against Mr. Bral is based on the premise that in holding such a crucial position . . . Mr. Bral was necessarily a leader in bringing about the work stoppages. The Company declares that . . . Mr. Bral had been aggressive in the opposition to the new schedule. . . . He is charged with making threats of what would happen if the Company placed the schedule into effect. The Company takes the position that at the meeting of the Union on Sunday he did not oppose the intention to refuse work assignments. The Company declares that Mr. Bral did nothing to prevent or deter the work stoppages that were taking place. . . . From the testimony it would seem that Mr. Bral did not take a prominent part in the Union meeting on Sunday, February 24. His testimony shows that he made no forthright statement . . . that the men must accept work assignments. . . . Instead, he refers to statements that the Company had the right to introduce the 20-turn schedule and that grievances could be carried through to arbitration. . . .

[14] *Ford Motor Co. and UAW*, Opinion A-153 (1944), in Shulman and Chamberlain, *Cases*, p. 432.

The record of his actions on February 25, 26 and 27 is similarly inconclusive. In substance he declares that while he was at work he had no contact with any individuals refusing their work assignments and that consequently he had no occasion to take action with reference to such work refusals. The Company has not challenged this testimony. The Company has not introduced evidence to show that Mr. Bral was in a position to act with regard to the work refusals and that he failed to do so. No connection has been established between Mr. Bral's actions and the work stoppage on Wednesday, February 27. . . .

Since no decisive showing has been made that Mr. Bral instigated, aided or condoned the work stoppages or that he failed to make reasonably expected efforts to prevent members of the Union from engaging in them, this Board finds no proper cause for his discharge. The Board rules that he be reinstated to employment and that he be recompensated for losses in his wages as a result of his suspension and discharge.[15]

How, then, is a union official in the plant to avoid the charge of instigating, aiding, or condoning a work stoppage? The answer is not too difficult, although action in line with it may be anything but easy during the confusion and high temper of a dispute with management. As to procedure:

1. He should counsel recourse to established grievance procedures rather than direct action.

2. He should advise, publicly and privately, the exhaustion of all legal remedies provided for in the agreement and in legislation, and warn his colleagues explicitly of the dangers of breach of the contract.

3. He should go on record in union meetings to this effect.

With respect to the dispute:

4. If the matter is within his jurisdiction, he should publicly and openly attempt to negotiate with management through the regular grievance procedure.

5. He should not threaten the employer with any form of direct action.

If, in spite of this, an interference with production impends:

6. He should try to stop it.

---

[15] Herbert Blumer, Chairman of Board of Arbitration, in *American Steel and Wire Co. and USWA* (1946), 5 LA 193, in Shulman and Chamberlain, *Cases,* p. 481.

7. He should notify his superior officers in the union—plant, local, and international—of the danger.

And if the stoppage occurs:

8. He should urge those taking part to return to work.

9. He should refrain from joining the picket line, except to attempt to persuade those forming it to abandon their activities. Evidence of failure to meet the above tests may be interpreted as instigation, aid, or condonation:

> Certainly, McCaw knew . . . that a strike was to begin on October 29. Yet he did nothing to prevent it, nor did he notify the district officials of the union. [He was] the highest officer of the local union (with knowledge of the situation). . . . And McCaw's failure to urge the members to return to work on October 29 or at the two meetings of the local union; his frequent picketing (alone) . . . and his reluctance at the hearing to relate all the facts of what occurred just prior to the strike indicate that McCaw did aid and abet the strike.[16]

Clear and sufficient evidence may be very difficult for management to come by, and management has the responsibility for enforcing discipline. The employer is not expected to be informed of what takes place at union meetings or in prestrike meetings of union representatives among themselves or with members. In the confusion of a work stoppage, supervision must rely on its interpretation of what it sees and hears and has reported to it. Where preparations are secret and unannounced, something less than direct and positive proof is sufficient. With respect to union officials, this may consist of:

a. being on hand at the time of stoppage, though not scheduled for work;

b. being openly opposed to the management action precipitating the walkout;

c. wearing picket armbands or other forms of identification;[17] *or*

d. prior knowledge of the time of walkout;

---

[16] Arbitrator Robert J. Wagner in *Pittsburgh Tube Co. and USWA* (1946), 1 LA 285.

[17] Hubert Wyckoff, Chairman of Board of Arbitration in *Bethlehem Steel Co. and USWA* (1947), 6 LA 617.

e. unusual actions in circulating among employees;

f. communication of the time set for the strike;

g. surreptitious signals given to employees.[18]

Where evidence is circumstantial, the circumstances must be proved and not based on supposition. In one case, the discharge of a union steward for starting a walkout was based mainly on the testimony of the company safety director who said that the man "made a gesture which indicated (according to his knowledge as a former union committeeman) that work is to cease." Under cross-examination, the safety director admitted: (1) that it was impossible to see the steward when he came into the room; (2) that he did not see the steward telling any employee or employees to stop working; (3) that the gesture used was the first within his knowledge; and (4) that he was basing his observations on supposition.[19]

A strike is misconduct of the most serious sort; appropriate penalties are the standard categories of warning, reprimand, suspension, and discharge.[20] Since striking has little or no relationship to work performance, the withholding of merit increases is unjustifiable as lacking a direct relationship between the offense and the penalty. An employer who held that all 41 employees of a department which had suffered a two-day work stoppage had forfeited their rights to merit increases was therefore reversed by the arbitrator. It was pointed out that the merit rating covered a period of four months, whereas the strike lasted only two days. The stoppage would not affect an employee's score on quality of work, quantity of work, adaptability, or job knowledge; the most that could be said was that it might reflect on the employee's dependability and attitude. It would therefore affect the total score only to a limited extent. It was also discriminatory, in that

---

[18] Arbitrator Whitley P. McCoy in *Stockham Pipe Fittings Co. and USWA* (1946), 4 LA 744.

[19] *Fruehauf Trailer Co. and UAW* (1944), 1 LA 155, Arbitrator A. C. Lappin, The steward was reinstated with pay and seniority for time lost. In the same case, the discharge of a committeeman of eight years seniority was upheld. Here the evidence was clear and convincing. In the presence of several supervisors, the committeeman had told the employees to put up their tools and go home.

[20] Fines are permissible as a method of recouping production losses due to deliberate limitation of output.

it fell mainly on the meritorious and did not take into account employees who did not take part because of absence for illness or other reasons.[21]

Inadequate evidence heads the list of reasons given by arbitrators for reversing or modifying penalties in strike and slowdown cases. Undue severity of the penalty and discrimination take second and third place. Together, these three account for 60 per cent of the cases in which arbitrators disagree with the judgment of management. The remainder show a wide dispersion, as follows:

ARBITRATORS' REASONS FOR REVERSAL OR MODIFICATION OF PENALTIES IN STRIKE OR SLOWDOWN CASES, VOLS. 1–10, LAR.[22]

Reasons for reversal	Number of cases
Inadequate evidence	16
Penalty too severe[a]	8
Discrimination	8
Extenuating circumstances: long service	5
Extenuating circumstances: management responsibility	4
Negative involvement (intimidation)	2
Extenuating circumstances: inexperience of union officials	2
Inappropriate penalty–withholding merit increases	1
Failure to consult with union on penalties	1
Extenuating circumstances: hazardous assignment	1
Extenuating circumstances: sympathetic strike	1
Failure to notify employes as required by contract	1
Strike settlement legitimatized action	1
Contract exemption—union to discipline its officials	1
Total	52

[a] Usually coupled with a judgment of lesser responsibility.

For what they are worth, the statistics of published awards in cases of alleged strike or instigation of strike or slowdown are presented in tables 16 and 17. The percentage of disciplinary actions upheld is about as usual, whereas the proportion of out-

[21] Arbitrator Benjamin S. Kirsh in *John Waldron Corp. and IAM* (1946), 5 LA 473.

[22] The reasoning of arbitrators is pluralistic, so selecting one reason out of several may seem unrealistic. However, there is often one reason which is given more weight than others; where the balance is even, the distortion is lessened by the fact of compensation. The reasons most frequently held to be primary are also very frequently cited as supporting.

TABLE 16

PENALTIES ASSIGNED IN STRIKE AND SLOWDOWN CASES

Penalties	Cases	
	Number	Per cent
Discharge..........................	72	76
Suspension........................	20	21
Fines..............................	2	2
No Merit Increases.................	1	1
Total..........................	95[a]	

SOURCE: *Labor Arbitration Reports*, Volumes 1–10, Bureau of National Affairs.
[a] Total disagrees with number of awards because of inclusion of more than one grievance in a single decision.

TABLE 17

ARBITRATORS' DECISIONS IN STRIKE AND SLOWDOWN CASES

Decisions	Cases	
	Number	Per cent
ALL TYPES		
Upheld............................	43	45
Modified..........................	35	37
Reversed..........................	17	18
Total..........................	95	
DISCHARGE CASES		
Upheld............................	30	42
Modified..........................	31	43
Reversed..........................	11	15
Total..........................	72	
SUSPENSION CASES		
Upheld............................	12	60
Modified..........................	4	20
Reversed..........................	4	20
Total..........................	20	

SOURCE: *Labor Arbitration Reports*, Volumes 1–10, Bureau of National Affairs.

right reversals is the lowest of any major form of dereliction. The figures are illustrative only, no claim of precision or adequacy as a sample being implied.

Improper Acts of Union Representatives

The essence of improper action by a union official in the plant is taking advantage of his official position to the neglect of his regular production work, or interfering with management or employees in a manner not contemplated in the agreement.[23] Most current agreements contain very extensive statements of the privileges and responsibilities of union representatives, the reciprocal obligations of the union and the company with respect to avoidance of coercion or discrimination, and the proper conduct of union affairs on company property. Much of this may seem redundant, in view of its coverage in the Labor Management Relations Act and state labor relations acts, but it is there nevertheless, often with reinforcing procedural requirements.

With many variations in detail, the agreements provide for union representation, specifying:

1. the classes of representatives (stewards, committeemen, chairmen, etc.);

2. the numbers in each class;

3. their geographical or other jurisdictions;

4. limitations (such as employment in the district represented, maximum time to be spent away from production work, etc.);

5. duties (representation of employees, investigation and processing of grievances);

6. privileges (freedom from regular work, pay for time spent on grievances, access to plant records, etc.); and

---

[23] A very few cases are put in this category on grounds of improper acts by management. These comprise any form of discipline imposed upon employees, for which the real reason is antiunion discrimination. In this type of case, the countercharge of the union assumes precedence over the original complaint by the company. There is no clear line of demarcation between this sort of dispute and a large number of other disciplinary actions. Especially when the grievant is a member of the official family, it is common practice for unions to add a charge of discrimination to any other defenses they may offer. The distinction is simply one of degree; where the claim of antiunion bias is so prominent as to overshadow the balance of the argument, the case is classed as above. Most disputes of this type originate with managerial discipline of union representatives on grounds that the latter have taken advantage of their position.

7. procedural requirements (clocking in and out with foremen, passes into other departments, etc.).

The contracts may also carry specific commitments by the union or management or both to avoid discrimination, coercion, or unfriendly acts such as hostile statements. They may set limits to the authority of either union or management representatives, and they very often prohibit solicitation of membership or dues by union representatives on company time.[24]

The big company-wide industrial agreements customarily have something to say about all or most of these matters, and very few contracts of any kind fail to touch upon some of them. All in all, the possibilities of infringement are numerous, either through oversight or from intent to cut corners. The limited number of such disputes appearing in published arbitration awards seems to indicate that matters are worked out better than might be expected, either in original accommodation or in grievance bargaining before arbitration.

There is a considerable variety in the list as a whole, although more than three-quarters of the cases fall into five categories. The table of violations as charged is given below.

The basic problem of discipline in this area is indicated by the

Improper Acts of Union Representatives, Vols. 1–10, LAR

Excessive absence from or neglect of production duties	9
Interference with supervision (countermanding orders, etc.)	9
Unsatisfactory work (incompetence or inefficiency)	7
Union solicitation or union business on company time	6
Coercion of nonunion employees	4
Expulsion from union, maintenance-of-membership agreement	1
Interference with management in grievance meetings	1
Discharge of former union official during probationary period	1
Posting in plant of "Creed of a Union Scab"	1
Failing to "clock out" before handling union business	1
Drinking on the job	1
Layoff for "economy"	1
False report of illness	1
Transfer on account of physical disability	1
Total	44

[24] See Commerce Clearing House, *Clauses*, pp. 555–593, 625–633, for sample clauses and a good summary discussion of "Conduct of Union Affairs" and "Grievance Procedure" provisions.

lengthy and complicated provisions of the agreement. The company expects union representatives to carry out promptly and efficiently their duties of representing employees, conferring with management, and investigating and processing grievances. It is often willing to pay for this service at the employee's regular rate for his job classification and may or may not set a limit to the time so spent. It ordinarily does not expect to pay for time spent on internal union affairs such as canvassing for dues or proselyting for new members, and it asks that the steward or committeeman draw the line short of interference with management in grievance work. When the union representative is not busy with questions of contract interpretation, the company expects him to work steadily and with reasonable efficiency at his regular job.

The company in turn has the duty of treating the union as a contracting party of equal status with management in the plant when its representatives are engaged in their official duties. It may not temporize, delay, nor treat the union officers as subordinates when they are acting for the union. If it does, the latter may act independently although this involves interference with management ordinarily amounting to insubordination. For example:

On August 19, 1947, three regular full-time committeemen were absent. . . . The Chairman of the Unit appointed three alternates and asked for their recognition . . . (under Sec. 12 of Art. VI of the Agreement, which provided that in the absence of a regular committeeman, "The Company will recognize an alternate committeeman designated by the Chairman of the Unit Committee") . . . The Chairman did not arbitrarily select the three alternates. He designated . . . the men who were entitled to be alternates . . . namely, the runners-up in the election.

When the Chairman informed Management of the designations he was told that the three men were on important jobs and that their withdrawal would slow down the lines. He replied that he had designated as alternates the men whom he was bound to designate and that he could not change the selection. Between two and three hours passed and Management still did not release the three alternates. The Chairman then went to the men, told them that he had designated them as alternates and asked them to assume their duties as such. The men complied. Thereafter, the Chairman was given a disciplinary lay-off of two days for countermanding Supervision's orders and the three alternates were not paid from the time they left their jobs. . . .

The company stood squarely on its right to discipline for counter-manding the orders of supervision; it presented no evidence to show that production was halted or slowed down. The umpire therefore concluded:

These cases involve . . . the duty of the Company to respect action falling primarily within the Union's domain. Section 12 imposed an absolute duty on the Company to recognize an alternate committee-man designated by the Chairman in the circumstances stated. The duty is no more qualified by considerations of inconvenience than is the duty of recognizing an elected committeeman. The refusal to respect the designation was wholly unjustified. . . . The award is that the disciplinary penalty imposed on the Chairman . . . be re-scinded with compensation for the time lost, and that the . . . [others] be paid for the balance of the day involved.[25]

At the same time, Shulman, in company with all other arbitra-tors, has been insistent upon the obligation of union representa-tives to limit the time away from production work to that required for discharging their duties under the agreement:

The committeeman is in honor bound to work at his job when not handling grievances. If he does not do so, he commits a dishonest act in violation of the Contract and in violation of the duties of his office. He is not entitled to be paid for time thus spent away from his job.[26]

This observation was made in connection with a dispute over the dockage of a committeeman for taking an excessive amount of time for grievance handling. Admitting that "the proper alloca-tion of a committeeman's time under Paragraph 20 (which gave to committeemen the privilege of spending as much time away from their jobs as was needed for the prompt handling of griev-ances) is a delicate problem of mutual concern to the Company and the Union," Shulman then reviewed the procedure followed by supervision:

When the foreman noted that X was away for about three hours, he ordered the dockage. He made no investigation of X's activities during that period. He made no inquiries from X himself. Because he did not

---

[25] Umpire Harry Shulman in *Ford Motor Co. and UAW*, Opinion A-250 (1948), in Shulman and Chamberlain, *Cases*, pp. 46–47.

[26] *Ford Motor Co. and UAW*, Opinion A-124 (1944), in Shulman and Cham-berlain, *Cases*, pp. 26–27.

know of any grievances that required further handling by X and because three hours seemed a long time in any event, he concluded, without inquiry, that X was improperly away from his job. . . . If, falsely pretending that he was handling grievances, X spent the three hours loafing or visiting with friends, he is not entitled to be paid for them. If on the other hand, he honestly spent the time in handling grievances, he is entitled to be paid even though three hours "seems too much to spend on two grievances." The amount of time taken merely creates a suspicion . . . a determination of what he did in fact could be made properly only after investigation and inquiry. . . . The award is that X be reimbursed for the three hours he was docked.

An issue of equal delicacy is the allowable limits of aggressive action (speech, gestures, etc.) by union representatives in their dealings with management over grievances. For example, if a shop steward describes an incentive plan to a foreman as "thieving and robbery," is management justified in giving him a warning notice? The union held, in appealing the action, that "without condoning the particular language used," an important principle was involved, namely: "that shop stewards must have the right to prosecute grievances aggressively and zealously in good faith without fear of personal reprisal." [27] It pointed out that, aside from the intemperate language, the steward's actions were correct; there was no interference with production, he was acting in good faith, and there were reasonable grounds for suspicion of the incentive system he criticized.

The company conceded the principle, but objected to its application in this instance, arguing that a steward is not "clothed with immunity for misstatements which reach to the point of slander, particularly when . . . made in a loud voice in the presence of other employees." In finding for the union and ordering the warning expunged from the records, the arbitrator indicated that the issue was very closely balanced in his own mind. Observing that "in union-management dealings it is not so clear what constitutes a slander," he raised an interesting point: "If, during a grievance meeting, a foreman clearly slandered the Union, what remedy would be available to the Union?"

On net balance the undersigned concludes that, although Schmidt's language was highly improper and irresponsible, the Company's rem-

[27] *Weston Electrical Instrument Corp.* and *Weston Employees' Union* (1952), 5 ALAA 69,063, Arbitrator Thomas J. Reynolds.

edy was not justified. To allow the warning notice to stand in this case would appear to establish a precedent that would be harder for the parties to live with than the possibility (probability?) that occasionally a loud-mouthed shop steward may over-step the bounds of orderliness and decorum.

There is no easy answer to the question of rights, duties, and responsibilities of union representatives in the plant, but there are some fairly definite boundaries to be observed, whether they are written into the agreement or left out of it. Employees covered by the agreement have a right to representation, the converse of which is the obligation of stewards and committeemen promptly to hear, investigate, and process grievances. This implies that they will be freed from other tasks when so needed. When acting in their official capacities, union representatives are on their own, taking their authority from the contract.[28] This creates a considerable immunity to discipline for acts that might otherwise be considered highly improper, extending to direct countermanding of orders of supervision in some cases. This immunity has very definite limits, however, which are dependent on such factors as: contract stipulations, customary practice of the parties, acts and attitudes of supervision, and the circumstances of the case. If discipline is imposed for exceeding these limits, management should take care to have "clean hands," [29] to act upon evidence, and to be scrupulous in its observance of procedural requirements.

What this all adds up to is that management and union representatives should try to understand and respect each other's problems, deal in good faith, treat disputed matters as judicially as possible, and—if they disagree—avoid recrimination and rely instead on the dispute machinery to settle matters. The evidence such as it is, indicates that this is exactly what takes place most of the time, with a very small residue of cases going to arbitration, wherein the parties charge each other with improper acts. (See tables 18 and 19.)

---

[28] Although it is proper for management to require notice of the transition through check-out passes issued by foremen. See *Ford Motor Co. and UAW*, Opinion A-124 (1944), in Shulman and Chamberlain, Cases, pp. 24–25.

[29] *International Harvester Co. and UAW* (1952), 5 ALAA 68,954, Arbitrator Ray L. Forrester, provides an example of a discharge for insubordination rescinded because of highhanded, arbitrary, and confused treatment by the superintendent of production and labor relations officers in interfering with a committeeman during his investigation of a grievance.

TABLE 18

PENALTIES ASSIGNED IN "IMPROPER ACTS" CASES

Penalties	Cases	
	Number	Per cent
Discharge.........................	38	87
Suspension........................	4	9
Transfer..........................	1	2
Fine.............................	1	2
Total..........................	44	

SOURCE: *Labor Arbitration Reports*, Volume 1–10, Bureau of National Affairs.

TABLE 19

ARBITRATORS' DECISIONS IN "IMPROPER ACTS" CASES

Decisions	Cases	
	Number	Per cent
ALL TYPES		
Upheld...........................	21	48
Modified..........................	11	25
Reversed..........................	12	27
Total..........................	44	
DISCHARGE CASES		
Upheld............................	17	45
Modified..........................	10	26
Reversed..........................	11	29
Total..........................	38	

Chapter VII | Discipline as a Function of Personnel Management

In the unionized firm, the right to discipline is still a prerogative of management. If relations with the union are good, there probably will be notification and consultation at each step of the process, whether called for in the contract or not. This does not preclude disagreement, but it minimizes the probability of it. In the absence of coöperation, with the parties dealing at arm's length, management initiates and the union challenges. In either case, if the issue cannot be compromised it goes to an independent third party for settlement, that is, to arbitration.

There are almost no data from which any kind of guess can be made as to the disposition of grievances during the steps in the procedure before arbitration, nor is there the remotest hint of the number of disciplinary actions—or other forms of contract interpretation—taken by management which never become the subject matter of a grievance, either because no exception is taken by the employees affected or because the union refuses to press the complaint.[1] The only information of a systematic nature that is available is the published arbitration awards in *Labor Arbitration Reports* and *American Labor Arbitration Awards,* and these are a sample the size and validity of which is unknown.

If arbitration awards are taken as a basis for judgment, two

---

[1] Until these two areas are explored, we will have no real knowledge of how labor agreements are administered, or, to put it another way, of personal administration in the unionized firm.

conclusions emerge: that discipline is an important function of personnel management, and that the administration of industrial discipline has left something to be desired. The first conclusion is derived from a number of surveys, supported by the comments of qualified observers, to the effect that "disputes over discipline comprise the largest single category of grievances." [2] For example, Professor Myers reports that the Federal Mediation and Conciliation Service made 999 appointments of *ad hoc* arbitrators during 1954, of which one-third were to decide disciplinary grievances.[3] A survey of 1,000 grievances from the records of the Labor Arbitration Tribunal of the American Arbitration Association showed the following distribution by subject matter:[4] 25 per cent concerned discipline; 21 per cent seniority problems; 12 per cent job evaluation and work assignments; 6 per cent arbitrability; 5 per cent overtime; 5 per cent vacations. (No other category more than 2 per cent.)

TABLE 20

PENALTIES ASSIGNED IN DISCIPLINARY CASES

Penalties	Cases	
	Number	Per cent
Discharge............................	556	77
Suspension..........................	137	19
Other...............................	32	4
Total...........................	725[a]	

SOURCE: *Labor Arbitration Reports*, Volumes 1–10, Bureau of National Affairs.
[a] Total disagrees with the number of awards because of the inclusion of more than one grievance in a single decision.

The second conclusion is based upon the decisions of arbitrators in disciplinary cases. Under a labor agreement, discipline may be applied only for "just cause." If published arbitration

---

[2] See above, chap v. The quotation is from A. Howard Myers, "Concepts of Industrial Discipline," *Ninth Annual Meeting of the National Academy of Arbitrators* (Washington: Bureau of National Affairs, 1956), p. 61.
[3] *Ibid.*
[4] J. Noble Braden, "From Conflict to Cooperation," *Proceedings of the Sixth Annual Labor Relations Conference* (Morgantown, W. Va.: Institute of Industrial Relations, University of West Virginia, 1956), pp. 46–47.

awards are any criterion, the administration of discipline often fails to meet this test. A very substantial majority of grievances over this issue succeed, either in whole or in part, and the majority increases as the severity of the punishment rises.[5] Discharge in particular has failed to stand up in almost two-thirds (63 per cent) of the cases (see tables 20 and 21).

The reasons for this set of results can be summarized rather briefly. They do not prove bad faith, intentional injustice, or anti-

Decisions	Number	Per cent
PENALTIES ASSIGNED IN DISCIPLINARY CASES, VOLS. 25–26, LAR		
Discharge	79	79
Suspension	12	12
Other	9	9
Total	100	
ARBITRATORS' DECISIONS IN DISCIPLINARY CASES: ALL TYPES		
Upheld	45	45
Modified	38	38
Reversed	17	17
Total	100	
ARBITRATORS' DECISIONS, BY TYPE OF PENALTY		
Discharge		
Upheld	35	44
Modified	32	41
Reversed	12	15
Total	79	
Suspension		
Upheld	8	67
Modified	3	25
Reversed	1	8
Total	12	
Other		
Upheld	2	22
Modified	3	33
Reversed	4	45
Total	9	

[5] The data supporting this judgment are for a limited period, the awards in Volumes 1–10, *Labor Arbitration Reports*, ranging in date from 1942 to 1948. It is entirely possible that experience since 1948 has been different, and at least one authority is on record to this effect. See Braden, *op. cit.*, p. 47, wherein, referring to a study showing the overruling of management by arbitrators, he says: "Today the result would be different. Why:—First the decisions of management and of arbitrators are affected by changes in the economic and political situation. Second because of better consideration and preparation before action is taken by management and in the handling of grievances as well as in arbitration." To check this conclusion, I made a survey of discipline and discharge cases in Volumes 25 and 26 of *Labor Arbitration Reports*, for the period 1955–1956. The results, covering 100 decisions, show some improvement, but nothing spectacular.

TABLE 21

ARBITRATORS' DECISIONS IN DISCIPLINARY CASES

Decisions	Cases	
	Number	Per cent
ALL TYPES		
Upheld...........................	295	41
Modified.........................	221	30
Reversed........................	209	29
Total.........................	725	
DISCHARGE CASES		
Upheld...........................	207	37
Modified.........................	202	36
Reversed........................	147	27
Total.........................	556	
SUSPENSION CASES		
Upheld...........................	71	52
Modified.........................	16	11
Reversed........................	50	37
Total.........................	137	
OTHER CASES		
Upheld...........................	17	53
Modified.........................	3	9
Reversed........................	12	38
Total.........................	32	

SOURCE: *Labor Arbitration Reports*, Volumes 1–10, Bureau of National Affairs.

union bias. Instead, for the most part, they are an indication of the difficulties encountered in moving from a unilateral, authoritarian system of discipline to a quite different framework of administration—that of discipline by "due process." Due process is simply a method of insuring that the rules of fair play are observed. The way that this is done is to set up a formal, public procedure with appropriate opportunities for challenge at key points. The employee is assured of adequate notice, a hearing, representation by counsel, and the right of appeal. For management, there are several benchmarks.

Proper grounds.—Where the employee's offense is clearly antisocial or inimical to the organization, the substantive charge presents few problems. However, if the proscribed activity is one that is ordinarily permissible elsewhere, there must be a formal prohibition, and this involves questions of rule adoption, consistency with the agreement, publication, and so on. The key problem in connection with the charge is usually substantiation—the nature and sufficiency of the evidence. Here the requirements of due process are much more rigorous than those customarily employed by management, and here is where many disciplinary actions fail.

Correct procedure.—Procedure is the heart of due process. It affects every step in the proceeding, from the observation or report of a rule violation to closing the record. Correct procedure is crucial to: (1) the accumulation of evidence, (2) the notification of the employee and/or the union, (3) arrangements for representation, (4) conduct of the preliminary hearing, (5) allowance for union investigation, (6) grievance negotiations, (7) presentation to the arbitrator, if called for, and (8) final settlement. It has many dimensions: customary practices, time limits, contract requirements, attitudes of courtesy or the contrary, and so on. Correct procedure means operating on the assumption that the employee is innocent until proved guilty and giving him every chance to defend himself. It is important because the machinery of enforcement is in the hands of management, with the latter acting in the capacity of both prosecutor and judge.

Appropriate penalties.—To meet the test of due process, the punishment should fit the crime ("We do not hang a man for a traffic violation"). The promiscuous use of discharge as a penalty has been a major failing of industrial discipline, which the large number of "modified" rulings by arbitrators attests. There is a sufficient range of restraints in the standard categories of warning, reprimand, suspension, and discharge for almost any purpose. Corrective discipline, through graduated penalties, is defensible both morally and practically. It need not go so far as a published "price list," but no disciplinary policy is complete without some attention to the relationship between the gravity of the offense and the severity of the punishment.

As a supplement to the above, management should keep in mind three other tests which are implicit in the idea of due process: condonation, discrimination, and extenuating circumstances. Discipline should be just, impartial, humane, but it should also be certain. An on-again, off-again application of standards of behavior is improper. It is not within the province of management to decide that an employee may be disciplined today but that the same offense may be passed over tomorrow or next week. The employer's interpretation of rules is a testimony to his judgment of their importance. An offense condoned may well amount to a rule repealed.

Condonation is a test for the individual employee. Consistency is a group test for the enforcement of discipline. Other things being equal, employees guilty of similar offenses should receive equal punishments. If one is punished and the other let go, or if the punishment is markedly different in the two cases, or if the penalty is related to something extraneous to the situation (production needs, for example), the result is discrimination. Any deviation from established practice—in charges, procedures, or in selection of penalties—should be based on an explicit differentiation of cases. The customary heading under which this occurs is "extenuating circumstances."

Circumstances alter cases. An extenuating circumstance is a factor in the situation which justifies reduction or cancellation of the penalty.[6] It may be long service on the part of the employee. It may be a prior record without blemish. It may be supervisory ineptness, carelessness, or inefficiency. It may be the attitudes of the parties or one of them: employee contrition, managerial harshness, or the like. It may be found in the work environment (failure of equipment or material) or lie outside (strain or worry on the part of the employee because of personal difficulties).

In general, the allowance for extenuating circumstances is an

---

[6] Of course, not all circumstances are mitigating; they may be aggravating. In such cases, more severe punishment will be justified.

attempt to introduce equity into the judgment. It amounts to modification of the rule where the rule strictly applied would be deficient on account of its generality. This is the most flexible element in the disciplinary pattern, and the one least capable of standardization. But it cannot be omitted from the account without an unfair result, and in many instances it will be controlling.

The above is what due process means for management. What it means to the employee has been well summarized by the vice president of the American Arbitration Association:

I refer to the changing concept of the worker's job, his right to employment, and the function of arbitration as an application to the field of industrial relations of the "due process" idea which is the basis of our concept of democratic living.

There was a time when a worker's job was a thing of the hour; he could be hired or fired at will, and his only right was to be paid for the hour he worked. Today, the job has become a thing of value, including not only a wage, but health and welfare benefits, holidays and vacation, bonuses, fringe benefits of all kinds, pensions, and in some industries, even supplementary unemployment insurance. Furthermore—and this, I think, is most significant—the worker has come to have what might be called a *property right* in his job. His wages and benefits generally accrue with seniority, which increases the value of his job as time goes on.

Like any other property holder in our free, democratic society, he cannot be deprived of his rights except by "due process." Just as the American citizen finds his personal and property rights protected by the "due process" clause and other provisions of the Constitution of the United States, so does the worker find his personal and property rights to his job defended in the "due process" of grievance machinery and arbitration. When we keep in mind the fact that the average employee spends half his waking hours at work, and that his whole life and the well-being of his family depend upon what happens on his job, the full significance of the extension of "due process" to industrial relations becomes apparent.[7]

---

[7] Braden, *op. cit.*, pp. 43–44. (Italics in the original.)

Arbitration Awards Cited

Alan Wood Steel Co., 3 LA 557
American Iron and Machine Works Co., 5 ALAA 69,134
American Liberty Oil Co., 5 ALAA 69,313
American Republics Corp., 5 ALAA 69,018
American Steel and Wire Co., 5 LA 193
American Transformer Co., 1 LA 456
Armour and Co., 9 LA 904
Atlantic Parachute Corp., 5 ALAA 69,185
Aviation Maintenance Corp., 8 LA 261
Bakelite Corp., 1 LA 227
Bauman Brothers Furn. Manufacturing Co., 10 LA 79
Belden Brick Co., 5 ALAA 69,203
Bell Aircraft Corp., 16 LA 234
Bethlehem Steel Co., 5 LA 578
Bethlehem Steel Co., 6 LA 617
Bethlehem Steel Co., 7 LA 483
Bethlehem Steel Co., 5 ALAA 68,943
Boston Sausage and Provision Co., 8 LA 483
Cameron Iron Works, Inc., 25 LA 295
Cannon Electric, 5 ALAA 68,995
Carnegie-Illinois Steel Corp., 5 LA 363
Chrysler Corp., 5 ALAA 68,974
Chrysler Corp., 5 ALAA 69,096
Chrysler Corp., 5 ALAA 69,129
Connecticut Power Co., 5 ALAA 68,962
Consolidated Vultee Aircraft Corp., 11 LA 7
Consolidated Western Steel Corp., 13 LA 721
Die Tool and Engineering Co., 3 LA 156
Dist. Lodge No. 727, IAM, 7 LA 231
Douglas Aircraft Co., Inc., 3 LA 598
E. I. du Pont de Nemours, 9 LA 345
Food Machinery and Chemical Corp., 5 ALAA 69,082
Foote Bros. Gear and Machinery Corp., 1 LA 561
Foote Bros. Gear and Machinery Corp., 13 LA 848
Ford Motor Co. (A-2, 1943)

Torrington Co., 1 LA 35
Turner Co., 5 ALAA 69,332
Uinta Oil Refining Co., 5 ALAA 69,204
Union Oil Company of California, 1955
Weston Electrical Instrument Corp., 5 ALAA 69,063

Index

147